The Collected Drawings of AUBREY BEARDSLEY

Caricature of Beardsley by Max Beerbohm, 1896.

The Collected Drawings

of AUBREY BEARDSLEY

WITH AN APPRECIATION BY
ARTHUR SYMONS

EDITED BY
BRUCE S. HARRIS

BOUNTY BOOKS
A DIVISION OF CROWN PUBLISHERS, INC.
NEW YORK

EDITOR'S INTRODUCTION

In THE COLLECTED DRAWINGS OF AUBREY BEARDSLEY we have tried to gather the drawings that best exemplify the various stages of the artist's career. Although only twenty-six when he died, Beardsley's six years of major creativity fall into several artistic periods. A complete catalogue of Beardsley's works compiled by Aymar Vallance and revised by Beardsley himself can be found at the back of this book. An asterisk to the left of a listing indicates that the drawing is reproduced in this book.

The drawings are in chronological order, with a few exceptions. Beardsley's major periods can be deduced from the form of his signature. The early works are mostly unsigned. From 1891 to 1892 he used his initials—A.V.B. In mid-1892, the period of *Morte D'Arthur* and *The Bon Mots*, he used a mark that shows a definite Japanese influence. This mark became progressively more graceful and sometimes accompanied a very rough looking A.B. in plain block capitals in a corner of the design.

During Beardsley's career he did two versions of the same subject or two drawings of similar themes; in these cases we have interrupted chronological order to make esthetic comparisons. We have tried to reproduce as much of the major work as possible. Every illustration of note for *Morte D'Arthur, Salome, Lysistrata, The Rape of the Lock,* and *Volpone* is reproduced here. In addition, we have included a large selection of juvenilia, work for "The Studio," "The Yellow Book," "The Savoy," his illustrations for *The Bon Mots*, and many interesting miscellaneous drawings.

This volume contains a selection of drawings originally published in a privately printed book entitled *Fifty Drawings by Aubrey Beardsley, Selected From The Collection of Mr. H. S. Nicols.* These pictures, never before published in a non-subscription volume, are now deemed to be forgeries by the best authorities on Beardsley's work. We have included them here for two reasons. First, it is interesting to note how the erotic element in the real Beardsley work can be exaggerated into semi-pornography in the Nichols' fakes. There can be little doubt in looking at the forgeries that they were meant to appeal to the appetite for privately printed erotica rather than to the collector of rare editions of artistic work. Secondly, after one compares the sham with the authentic, one's admiration for Beardsley's technique increases tremendously. The fakes appear gross and clumsy whereas the genuine art, even when dealing with sexuality, reflects delicacy, grace, and taste.

Aubrey Beardsley's emphasis of the erotic element is present in almost every drawing, but nowhere as bold as in illustrations for *Lysistrata,* which were intended for a privately printed edition at a time when Beardsley was completely out of favor with polite society. One of his very last acts, congruent with his conversion to Roman Catholicism, was to write a letter to his not very respectable publisher, Leonard Smithers, in which he says: "I implore you to destroy *all* copies to Lysistrata and bad drawings....By all that is holy *all* obscene drawings." Smithers not only disregarded this plea, but continued to sell privately printed reproductions and trafficked in forgeries of these and other Beardsley subjects.

The essay by Arthur Symons combines a critique of Beardsley's art with a personal reminiscence. In evaluating Beardsley, more so than in the case of many artists, an understanding of his personality is extremely important and is necessary to a full appreciation of his art.

For the rest we have decided to let the work of Aubrey Beardsley speak for itself. The only other illustration not from Beardsley's pen is the famous caricature by Max Beerbohm. There can be no better introduction to Beardsley's work than Beerbohm's tribute to his friend:

> Aubrey Beardsley was famous in his youth, the most gracious gift that the gods can bestow. He died, having achieved masterpieces, at an age when normal genius has as yet done little of which it will not be heartily ashamed thereafter.

—BRUCE S. HARRIS

AUBREY BEARDSLEY: AN APPRECIATION
by Arthur Symons

IT was in the summer of 1895 that I first met Aubrey Beardsley. A publisher had asked me to form and edit a new kind of magazine, which was to appeal to the public equally in its letterpress and its illustrations: need I say that I am defining The Savoy? It was, I admit, to have been something of a rival to The Yellow Book, which had by that time ceased to mark a movement, and had come to be little more than a publisher's magazine. I forget exactly when the expulsion of Beardsley from The Yellow Book had occurred; it had been sufficiently recent, at all events, to make Beardsley singularly ready to fall in with my project when I went to him and asked him to devote himself to illustrating my quarterly. He was supposed, just then, to be dying; and as I entered the room, and saw him lying out on a couch, horribly white, I wondered if I had come too late. He was full of ideas, full of enthusiasm, and I think it was then that he suggested the name Savoy, finally adopted after endless changes and uncertainties.

A little later we met again at Dieppe, where for a month I saw him daily. It was at Dieppe that The Savoy was really planned, and it was in the café, which Sickert has so often painted, that I wrote the slightly pettish and defiant "Editorial Note", which made so many enemies for the first number. Dieppe just then was a meeting-place for the younger generation; some of us spent the whole summer there, lazily but profitably; others came and went. Beardsley at that time imagined himself to be unable to draw anywhere but in London. He made one or two faint attempts, and even prepared a canvas for a picture which was never painted, in the hospitable studio in which Jacques Blanche painted the admirable portrait which now remains with us. But he found many subjects, some of which he afterwards worked out, in the expressive opportunities of the Casino and the beach. He never walked; I never saw him look at the sea; but at night he was almost always to be seen watching the gamblers at *petits chevaux*, studying them with a sort of hypnotised attention for that picture of *The Little Horses*, which was never done. He liked the large deserted rooms, at hours when no one was there; the sense of frivolous things caught at a moment of suspended life, *en déshabille*. He would glance occasionally, but with more impatience, at the dances, especially the children's dances, in the concert room; but he rarely missed a concert, and would glide in every afternoon, and sit on the high benches at the side, always carrying his large, gilt-leather portfolio with the magnificent, old, red-lined folio paper, which he would often open, to write some

lines in pencil. He was at work then, with an almost pathetic tenacity, at his story, never to be finished, the story which never could have been finished, *Under the Hill*, a new version, a parody (like Laforgue's parodies, but how unlike them, or anything!) of the story of Venus and Tannhäuser. Most of it was done at these concerts, and in the little, close writing-room, where visitors sat writing letters. The fragment published in the first two numbers of The Savoy had passed through many stages before it found its way there, and would have passed through more if it had ever been carried further. Tannhäuser, not quite willingly, had put on Abbé's disguise, and there were other unwilling disguises in those brilliant, disconnected, fantastic pages, in which every sentence was meditated over, written for its own sake, and left to find its way in its own paragraph. It could never have been finished, for it had never really been begun; but what undoubted, singular, literary ability there is in it, all the same!

I think Beardsley would rather have been a great writer than a great artist; and I remember, on one occasion, when he had to fill up a form of admission to some library to which I was introducing him, his insistence on describing himself as "man of letters". At one time he was going to write an essay on *Les Liaisons Dangereuses*, at another he had planned a book on Rousseau. But his plans for writing changed even more quickly than his plans for doing drawings, and with less profitable results in the meantime. He has left no prose except that fragment of a story; and in verse only the three pieces published in The Savoy. Here, too, he was terribly anxious to excel; and his patience over a medium so unfamiliar, and hence so difficult, to him as verse, was infinite. We spent two whole days on the grassy ramparts of the old castle at Arques-la-Bataille, near Dieppe; I working at something or other in one part, he working at *The Three Musicians* in another. The eight stanzas of that amusing piece of verse are really, in their own way, a *tour de force*; by sheer power of will, by deliberately saying to himself, "I will write a poem," and by working with such strenuous application that at last a certain result, the kind of result he had willed, did really come about, he succeeded in doing what he had certainly no natural aptitude for doing. How far was that more genuine aspect of his genius also an "infinite capacity for taking pains"?

It was on the balcony of the Hôtel Henri IV at Arques, one of those September evenings, that I had the only quite serious, almost solemn, conversation I ever had with Beardsley. Not long before we had gone together to visit Alexandre Dumas *fils* at Puy, and it was from talking thoughtfully, but entirely, of that Parisian writer, and his touching, in its unreal way so real, *Dame aux Caméllias* (the novel, not the play), which Beardsley admired so much, that we passed into an unexpectedly intimate mood of speculation. Those stars up yonder, whether they were really the imprisoning worlds of other creatures like ourselves; the strange ways by which the soul might have come and must certainly go; death and the future: it was of such things that I found him speaking, for once without mockery. And he told me then a singular dream or vision which he had had when a child, waking up at night in the moonlight and seeing a great cruicfix, with a bleeding Christ, falling off the wall, where certainly there was not, and had never been, any crucifix. It is only by remembering that one conversation, that vision, the tone of awe with which he told it, that I can, with a great effort, imagine to myself the Beardsley whom I knew, with his so positive intelligence, his imaginative sight of the very spirit of man as a thing of definite outline, transformed finally into the Beardsley who died in the peace of the last sacraments, holding the rosary between his fingers.

Anima naturaliter pagana, Aubrey Beardsley ended a long career, at the age of twenty-six, in the arms of the Church. No artist of our time, none certainly whose work has been in black and white, has reached a more universal, or a more contested fame; none has formed for himself, out of such alien elements, a more personal originality of manner; none has had so wide an influence on contemporary art. He had the fatal speed of those who are to die young; that disquieting completeness and extent of knowledge, that absorption of a lifetime in an hour, which we find in those who hasten to have done their work before noon, knowing that they will not see the evening. He had played the piano in drawing-rooms as an infant prodigy, before, I suppose, he had ever drawn a line; famous at twenty as a draughtsman, he found time, in those incredibly busy years which remained to him, deliberately to train himself into a writer of prose which was, in its way, as original as his draughtsmanship, and into a writer of verse which had at least ingenious and original moments. He seemed to have read everything, and had his preferences as adroitly in order, as wittily in evidence, as almost any man of letters; indeed, he seemed to know more, and was a sounder critic, of books than of pictures; with perhaps a deeper feeling for music than for either. His conversation had a peculiar kind of brilliance, different in order but scarcely inferior in quality to that of any other contemporary master of that art; a salt, whimsical dogmatism, equally full of convinced egoism and of imperturbable keen-sightedness. Generally choosing to be paradoxical, and vehement on behalf of any enthusiasm of the mind, he was the dupe of none of his own statements, or indeed of his own enthusiasms, and, really, very coldly impartial.

I scarcely except even his own judgment of himself, in spite of his petulant, amusing self-assertion, so full of the childishness of genius. He thought, and was right in thinking, very highly of himself; he admired himself enormously; but his intellect would never allow itself to be deceived even about his own accomplishments.

This clear, unemotional intellect, emotional only in the perhaps highest sense, where emotion almost ceases to be recognisable, in the abstract, for ideas, for lines, left him, with all his interests in life, with all his sociability, of a sort, essentially very lonely. Many people were devoted to him, but he had, I think, scarcely a friend, in the fullest sense of the word; and I doubt if there were more than one or two people for whom he felt any real affection. In spite of constant ill-health, he had an astonishing tranquillity of nerves; and it was doubtless that rare quality which kept him, after all, alive so long. How far he had deliberately acquired command over his nerves and his emotions, as he deliberately acquired command over his brain and hand, I do not know. But there it certainly was, one of the bewildering characteristics of so contradictory a temperament.

One of his poses, as people say, one of those things, that is, in which he was most sincere, was his care in outwardly conforming to the conventions which make for elegance and restraint; his necessity of dressing well, of showing no sign of the professional artist. He had a great contempt for what seemed to inferior craftsmen, inspiration, for what I have elsewhere called the plenary inspiration of first thoughts; and he hated the outward and visible signs of an inward yeastiness and incoherency. It amused him to denounce everything, certainly, which Baudelaire would have denounced; and, along with some mere *gaminerie*, there was a very serious and adequate theory of art at the back of all his destructive criticisms. It was a profound thing which he said to a friend of mine who asked him whether he ever saw visions: "No," he replied, "I do not allow myself to see them except on paper". All his art is in that phrase.

And he attained, to the full, one certainly of his many desires, and that one, perhaps, of which he was most keenly or most continuously conscious: contemporary fame, the fame of a popular singer or a professional beauty, the fame of Yvette Guilbert or of Cléo de Mérode. And there was logic in his insistence on this point, in his eagerness after immediate and clamorous success. Others might have waited; he knew that he had not the time to wait. After all, posthumous fame is not a very cheering prospect to look forward to, on the part of those who have worked without recompense, if the pleasure or the relief of work is not enough in itself. Every artist has his own secret, beyond the obvious one, of why he works. So far as it is not the mere need of earning one's living, it is generally some unhappiness, some dissatisfaction with the things about one, some too desperate or too contemptuous sense of the meaning of existence. At one period of his life a man works at his art to please a woman; then he works because he has not pleased the woman; and then because he is tired of pleasing her. Work for the work's sake it always must be, in a profound sense; and with Beardsley, not less certainly than with Blake or with Rossetti. But that other, that accidental, insidious, significant motive, was, with Beardsley, the desire to fill his few working years with the immediate echo of a great notoriety.

Like most artists who have thought much of popularity, he had an immense contempt for the public; and the desire to kick it for admiring the wrong thing or not knowing why it was admiring, led him into many of his most outrageous practical jokes of the pen. He was partly right and partly wrong, for he was indiscriminate; and to be indiscriminate is always to be partly right and partly wrong. The wish to *épater le bourgeois* is a natural one, and though a little beside the question, does not necessarily lead one astray. The general public, of course, does not in the least know why it admires the right thing to-day though it admired the wrong thing yesterday. But there is such a thing as denying your Master while you are rebuking a servant-girl. Beardsley was without the very sense of respect; it was one of his limitations.

And this limitation was an unfortunate one, for it limited his ambition. With the power of creating beauty, which should be pure beauty, he turned aside, only too often, to that lower kind of beauty which is the mere beauty of technique, in a composition otherwise meaningless, trivial, or grotesque. Saying to himself, "I can do what I like; there is nothing I could not do if I chose to, if I chose to take the trouble; but why should I offer hard gold when an I.O.U. will be just the same? I can pay up whenever the money is really wanted", he allowed himself to be content with what he knew would startle, doing it with infinite pains, to his own mind conscientiously, but doing it with that lack of reverence for great work which is one of the most sterilising characteristics of the present day.

The epithet *fin de siècle* has been given, somewhat loosely, to a great deal of modern French art, and to art which, in one way or another, seems to attach itself to contemporary France. Out of the great art of Manet, the serious art of Degas, the exquisite art of Whistler, all, in such different ways, so modern, there has come into existence a new, very modern, very far from great or serious or really exquisite kind of art, which has expressed itself largely in the *Courrier Français*, the *Gil Blas Illustré*, and the posters. All this art may be said to be, what the quite new art of the poster certainly is, art meant for the street, for people who are walking fast. It comes into competition with the newspapers, with the music halls; half contemptuously, it popularises itself; and, with real qualities and a real measure of good inten-

tion, finds itself forced to seek for sharp, sudden, arresting means of expression. Instead of seeking pure beauty, the seriousness and self-absorption of great art, it takes, wilfully and for effect, that beauty which is least evident, indeed least genuine; nearest to ugliness in the grotesque, nearest to triviality in a certain elegant daintiness, nearest also to brutality and the spectacular vices. Art is not sought for its own sake, but the manual craftsman perfects himself to express a fanciful, ingenious, elaborate, somewhat tricky way of seeing things, which he has deliberately adopted. It finds its own in the eighteenth century, so that Willette becomes a kind of petty, witty Watteau of Montmartre; it parodies the art of stained glass with Grasset and his followers; it juggles with iron bars and masses of shadow, like Lautrec. And in its direct assault on the nerves, it pushes naughtiness to obscenity, deforms observation into caricature, dexterity of line and handling being cultivated as one cultivates a particular, deadly *botte* in fencing.

And this art, this art of the day and hour, competes not merely with the appeal and the popularity of the theatrical spectacle, but directly with theatrical methods, the methods of stage illusion. The art of the ballet counts for much in the evolution of many favourite effects of contemporary drawing, and not merely because Degas has drawn dancers, with his reserved, essentially classical mastery of form. By its rapidity of flight within bounds, by its bird-like and flower-like caprices of colour and motion, by that appeal to the imagination which comes from its silence (to which music is but like an accompanying shadow, so closely, so discreetly, does it follow the feet of the dancers), by its appeal to the eyes and to the senses, its adorable artificiality, the ballet has tempted almost every draughtsman, as the interiors of music-halls have also been singularly tempting, with their extraordinary tricks of light, their suddenness of gesture, their triumphant tinsel, their fantastic humanity. And pantomime, too, in the French and correct, rather than in the English and incorrect, sense of that word, has had its significant influence. In those pathetic gaieties of Willette, in the windy laughter of the frivolities of Chéret, it is the masquerade, the English clown or acrobat seen at the Folies-Bergère, painted people mimicking puppets, who have begotten this masquerading humanity of posters and illustrated papers. And the point of view is the point of view of Pierrot—

"le subtil génie
De sa malice infinie
De poète-grimacier"—

Verlaine's *Pierrot gamin*.

Pierrot is one of the types of our century, of the moment in which we live, or of the moment, perhaps, out of which we are just passing. Pierrot is passionate; but he does not believe in great passions. He feels himself to be sickening with a fever, or else perilously convalescent; for love is a disease, which he is too weak to resist or endure. He has worn his heart on his sleeve so long, that it has hardened in the cold air. He knows that his face is powdered, and if he sobs, it is without tears; and it is hard to distinguish, under the chalk, if the grimace which twists his mouth awry is more laughter or mockery. He knows that he is condemned to be always in public, that emotion would be supremely out of keeping with his costume, that he must remember to be fantastic if he would not be merely ridiculous. And so he becomes exquisitely false, dreading above all things that "one touch of nature" which would ruffle his disguise, and leave him defenceless. Simplicity, in him being the most laughable thing in the world, he becomes learned, perverse, intellectualising his pleasures, brutalising his intellect; his mournful contemplation of things becoming a kind of grotesque joy, which he expresses in the only symbols at his command, tracing his Giotto's O with the elegance of his pirouette.

And Beardsley, with almost more than the Parisian's deference to Paris, and to the moment, was, more than any Parisian, this *Pierrot gamin*. He was more than that, but he was that: to be that was part of what he learnt from France. It helped him to the pose which helped him to reveal himself; as Burne-Jones had helped him when he did the illustrations to the *Morte d'Arthur*, as Japanese art helped him to free himself from that influence, as Eisen and Saint-Aubin showed him the way to the *Rape of the Lock*. He had that originality which surrenders to every influence, yet surrenders to absorb, not to be absorbed; that originality which, constantly shifting, is true always to its centre. Whether he learnt from M. Grasset or from Mr. Ricketts, from an 1830 fashion-plate, or from an engraved plate by Hogarth, whether the scenery of Arques-la-Bataille composed itself into a pattern in his mind, or, in the Casino at Dieppe, he made a note of the design of a looped-up window-blind, he was always drawing to himself, out of the order of art or the confusion of natural things, the thing he wanted, the thing he could make his own. And he found, in the French art of the moment, a joyous sadness, the service to God of Mephistopheles, which his own temperament and circumstances were waiting to suggest to him.

"In more ways than one do men sacrifice to the rebellious angels," says St. Augustine; and Beardsley's sacrifice, together with that of all great decadent art, the art of Rops or the art of Baudelaire, is really a sacrifice to the eternal beauty, and only seemingly to the powers of evil. And here let me say that I have no concern with what neither he nor I could have had absolute knowledge of, his own intention in his work. A man's intention, it must be remembered, from the very fact that it is conscious, is much less intimately himself than the sentiment which his work conveys to me. So large is the sub-conscious element in all

artistic creation, that I should have doubted whether Beardsley himself knew what he intended to do, in this or that really significant drawing. Admitting that he could tell exactly what he had intended, I should be quite prepared to show that he had really done the very contrary. Thus when I say he was a profoundly spiritual artist, though seeming to care chiefly for the manual part of his work; that he expresses evil with an intensity which lifted it into a region almost of asceticism, though attempting, not seldom, little more than a joke or a caprice in line; and that he was above all, though almost against his own will, a satirist, a satirist who has seen the ideal,—I am putting forward no paradox, nothing really contradictory, but a simple analysis of the work as it exists.

At times he attains pure beauty, has the unimpaired vision; in the best of the *Salome* designs, here and there afterwards. From the first it is a diabolic beauty, but it is not yet divided against itself. The consciousness of sin is always there, but it is sin first transfigured by beauty, and then disclosed by beauty; sin, conscious of itself, of its inability to escape itself, and showing in its ugliness the law it has broken. His world is a world of phantoms, in whom the desire of the perfecting of mortal sensations, a desire of infinity, has overpassed mortal limits, and poised them, so faint, so quivering, so passionate for flight, in a hopeless and strenuous immobility. They have the sensitiveness of the spirit, and that bodily sensitiveness which wastes their veins and imprisons them in the attitude of their luxurious meditation. They are too thoughtful to be ever really simple, or really absorbed by either flesh or spirit. They have nothing of what is "healthy" or merely "animal" in their downward course towards repentance; no overwhelming passion hurries them beyond themselves; they do not capitulate to an open assault of the enemy of souls. It is the soul in them that sins, sorrowfully, without reluctance, inevitably. Their bodies are faint and eager with wantonness; they desire more pleasure than there is in the world, fiercer and more exquisite pains, a more intolerable suspense. They have put off the common burdens of humanity, and put on that loneliness which is the rest of saints and the unrest of those who have sinned with the intellect. They are a little lower than the angels, and they walk between these and the fallen angels, without part or lot in the world.

Here, then, we have a sort of abstract spiritual corruption, revealed in beautiful form; sin transfigured by beauty. And here, even if we go no further, is an art intensely spiritual, an art in which evil purifies itself by its own intensity, and by the beauty which transfigures it. The one thing in the world which is without hope is that mediocrity which is the sluggish content of inert matter. Better be vividly awake to evil than, in mere somnolence, close the very issues and approaches of good and evil. For evil itself, carried to the point of a perverse ecstasy, becomes a kind of good, by means of that energy which, otherwise directed, is virtue; and which can never, no matter how its course may be changed, fail to retain something of its original efficacy. The devil is nearer to God, by the whole height from which he fell, than the average man who has not recognised his own need to rejoice or repent. And so a profound spiritual corruption, instead of being a more "immoral" thing than the gross and pestiferous humanity of Hogarth or of Rowlandson, is more nearly, in the final and abstract sense, moral, for it is the triumph of the spirit over the flesh, to no matter what end. It is a form of divine possession, by which the inactive and materialising soul is set in fiery motion, lured from the ground, into at least a certain high liberty. And so we find evil justified of itself, and an art consecrated to the revelation of evil equally justified; its final justification being that declared by Plotinus, in his treatise *On the Nature of Good and Evil:* "But evil is permitted to remain by itself alone on account of the superior power and nature of good; because it appears from necessity everywhere comprehended and bound, in beautiful bands, like men fettered with golden chains, lest it should be produced openly to the view of divinity, or lest mankind should always behold its horrid shape when perfectly naked; and such is the supervening power of good, that whenever a glimpse of perfect evil is obtained we are immediately recalled to the memory of good by the image of the beautiful with which evil is invested."

In those drawings of Beardsley which are grotesque rather than beautiful, in which lines begin to grow deformed, the pattern, in which now all the beauty takes refuge, is itself a moral judgment. Look at that drawing called *The Scarlet Pastorale.* In front, a bloated harlequin struts close to the footlights, outside the play, on which he turns his back; beyond, sacramental candles have been lighted, and are guttering down in solitude, under an unseen wind. And between, on the sheer darkness of the stage, a bald and plumed Pierrot, holding in his vast, collapsing paunch with a mere rope of roses, shows the cloven foot, while Pierrette points at him in screaming horror, and the fat dancer turns on her toes indifferently. Need we go further to show how much more than Gautier's meaning lies in the old paradox of *Mademoiselle de Maupin*, that "perfection of line is virtue"? That line which rounds the deformity of the cloven-footed sin, the line itself, is at once the revelation and the condemnation of vice, for it is part of that artistic logic which is morality.

Beardsley is the satirist of an age without convictions, and he can but paint hell as Baudelaire did, without pointing for contrast to any contemporary paradise. He employs the same rhetoric as Baudelaire, a method of emphasis which it is uncritical to think insincere. In that terrible annunciation of evil which he called *The Mysterious Rose-Garden*, the lantern-bearing angel with winged sandals whispers, from among the falling roses, tidings of more than

"pleasant sins". The leering dwarfs, the "monkeys" by which the mystics symbolised the earthlier vices; those immense bodies swollen with the lees of pleasure, and those cloaked and masked desires shuddering in gardens and smiling ambiguously at interminable toilets; are part of a symbolism which loses nothing by lack of emphasis. And the peculiar efficacy of this satire is that it is so much the satire of desire returning upon itself, the mockery of desire enjoyed, the mockery of desire denied. It is because he loves beauty that beauty's degradation obsesses him; it is because he is supremely conscious of virtue that vice has power to lay hold upon him. And, unlike those other, acceptable satirists of our day, with whom satire exhausts itself in the rebuke of a drunkard leaning against a lamp-post, or a lady paying the wrong compliment in a drawing-room, he is the satirist of essential things; it is always the soul, and not the body's discontent only, which cries out of these insatiable eyes that have looked on all their lusts, and out of these bitter mouths that have eaten the dust of all their sweetness, and out of these hands that have laboured delicately for nothing, and out of these feet that have run after vanities. They are so sorrowful because they have seen beauty, and because they have departed from the line of beauty.

And after all, the secret of Beardsley is there; in the line itself rather than in anything, intellectually realised, which the line is intended to express. With Beardsley everything was a question of form: his interest in his work began when the paper was before him and the pen in his hand. And so, in one sense, he may be said never to have known what he wanted to do, while, in another, he knew very precisely indeed. He was ready to do, within certain limits, almost anything you suggested to him; as, when left to himself, he was content to follow the caprice of the moment. What he was sure of, was his power of doing exactly what he proposed to himself to do; the thing itself might be *Salome* or *Belinda*, *Ali Baba* or *Réjane*, the *Morte d'Arthur* or the *Rhinegold* or *Les Liaisons Dangereuses;* the design might be for an edition of a classic or for the cover of a catalogue of second-hand books. And the design might seem to have no relation with the title of its subject, and indeed, might have none: its relation was of line to line within the limits of its own border, and to nothing else in the world. Thus he could change his whole manner of working five or six times over in the course of as many years, seem to employ himself much of the time on trivial subjects, and yet retain, almost unimpaired, an originality which consisted in the extreme beauty and the absolute certainty of design.

It was a common error, at one time, to say that Beardsley could not draw. He certainly did not draw the human body with any attempt at rendering its own lines, taken by themselves; indeed, one of his latest drawings, an initial letter to *Volpone*, is almost the first in which he has drawn a nude figure realistically. But he could draw, with extraordinary skill, in what is after all the essential way: he could make a line do what he wanted it to do, express the conception of form which it was his intention to express; and this is what the conventional draughtsman, Bouguereau, for instance, cannot do. The conventionl draughtsman, any Academy student, will draw a line which shows quite accurately the curve of a human body, but all his science of drawing will not make you feel that line, will not make that line pathetic, as in the little, drooping body which a satyr and a Pierrot are laying in a puff-powder coffin, in the tailpiece to *Salome*.

And then, it must never be forgotten, Beardsley was a decorative artist, and not anything else. From almost the very first he accepted convention; he set himself to see things as pattern. Taking freely all that the Japanese could give him, that release from the bondage of what we call real things, which comes to one man from an intense spirituality, to another from a consciousness of material form so intense that it becomes abstract, he made the world over again in his head, as if it existed only when it was thus re-made, and not even then, until it had been set down in black line on a white surface, in white line on a black surface. Working, as the decorative artist must work, in symbols almost as arbitrary, almost as fixed, as the squares of a chess-board, he swept together into his pattern all the incongruous things in the world, weaving them into congruity by his pattern. Using the puff-box, the toilet-table, the ostrich-feather hat, with a full consciousness of their suggestive quality in a drawing of archaic times, a drawing purposely fantastic, he put these things to beautiful uses, because he liked their forms, and because his space of white or black seemed to require some such arrangement of lines. They were the minims and crotchets by which he wrote down his music; they made the music, but they were not the music.

In the *Salome* drawings, in most of The Yellow Book drawings, we see Beardsley under this mainly Japanese influence; with, now and later, in his less serious work, the but half-admitted influence of what was most actual, perhaps most temporary, in the French art of the day. *Pierrot gamin*, in *Salome* itself, alternates, in such irreverences as the design of *The Black Cape*, with the creator of noble line, in the austere and terrible design of *The Dancer's Reward*, the ornate and vehement design of *The Peacock Skirt*. Here we get pure outline, as in the frontispiece; a mysterious intricacy, as in the border of the title-page and of the table of contents; a paradoxical beauty of mere wilfulness, but a wilfulness which has its

meaning, its excuse, its pictorial justification, as in *The Toilette*. The Yellow Book embroiders upon the same manner; but in the interval between the last drawings for The Yellow Book and the first drawings for The Savoy, a new influence has come into the work, the influence of the French eighteenth century. This influence, artificial as it is, draws him nearer, though somewhat unquietly nearer, to nature. Drawings like *The Fruit Bearers*, in the first number of The Savoy, with its solid and elaborate richness of ornament, or *The Coiffing*, in the third number, with its delicate and elaborate grace, its witty concentration of line: drawings like the illustrations to the *Rape of the Lock* have, with less extravagance and also a less strenuous intellectual effort, a new mastery of elegant form, not too far removed from nature while still subordinated to the effect of decoration, to the instinct of line. In the illustrations to Ernest Dowson's *Pierrot of the Minute*, we have a more deliberate surrender, for the moment, to Eisen and Saint-Aubin, as yet another manner is seen working itself out. The illustrations to *Mademoiselle de Maupin*, seemed to me when I first saw them, with the exception of one extremely beautiful design in colour, to show a certain falling off in power, an actual weakness in the handling of the pen. But in their not quite successful feeling after natural form, they did but represent, as I afterwards found, the moment of transition to what must now remain for us, and may well remain, Beardsley's latest manner. The four initial letters to *Volpone*, the last of which was finished not more than three weeks before his death, have a new quality both of hand and of mind. They are done in pencil, and they lose, as such drawings are bound to lose, very greatly in the reduced reproduction. But in the original they are certainly, in sheer technical skill, equal to anything he had ever done, and they bring at the last, and with complete success, nature itself into the pattern. And here, under some solemn influence, the broken line of beauty has reunited; "the care is over," and the trouble has gone out of this no less fantastic world, in which Pan still smiles from his terminal column among the trees, but without the old malice. Human and animal form reassert themselves, with a new dignity, under this new respect for their capabilities. Beardsley has accepted the convention of nature itself, turning it to his own uses, extracting from it his own symbols, but no longer rejecting it for a convention entirely of his own making. And thus in his last work, done under the very shadow of death, we find new possibilities for an art, conceived as pure line, conducted through mere pattern which, after many hesitations, has resolved finally upon the great compromise, that compromise which the greatest artists have made between the mind's outline and the outline of visible things.

Frontispiece to *Ghosts*.

A Scene from
Manon Lescaut.

Hail Mary.
Pencil Sketch.

Frontispiece to Balzac's
Contes Drôlatiques.

Francesca Di Rimini (Dante)

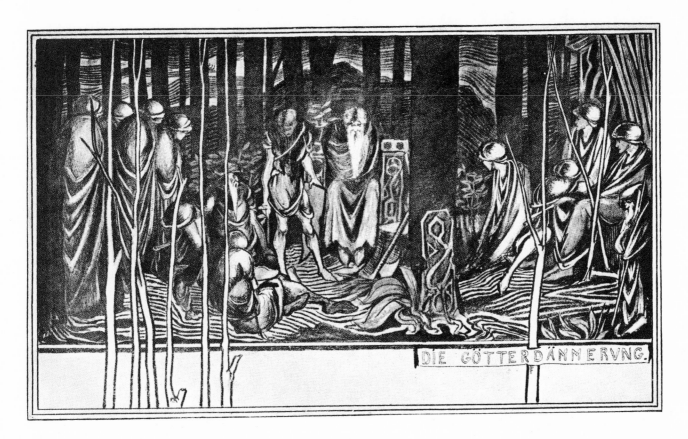

Die Götterdämmerung.

Aeneid:
"All night I lay hid in a weedy lake."

Aeneid:
The Palladium is snatched away.

Aeneid:
The Palladium jumpeth.

Aeneid:
Laocoon sacrificeth on the sand.

Aeneid:
Æneas heareth the clash of arms.

Aeneid:
Death of Priam.

Aeneid:
Æneas debateth whether he shall slay Helen.

Aeneid:
Venus appeareth to Æneas.

Aeneid:
Jupiter hurls the lighting.

Aeneid:
Æneas and company set out from Troy.

Soleil Couchant.

9

Withered Spring.

Hamlet. From *The Bee* magazine,
December, 1892.

A Book-Mark.

The Litany of Mary Magdalen.

A Portrait of Aubrey Beardsley by Himself.

Sandro Botticelli.

15

"Siegfried." From *The Studio*.

Cover Design. From *Le Morte D'Arthur*.

THE BIRTH LIFE AND ACTS OF KING ARTHUR OF HIS
NOBLE KNIGHTS OF THE ROUND TABLE THEIR
MARVELLOUS ENQUESTS AND ADVENTURES
THE ACHIEVING OF THE SAN GREAL
AND IN THE END LE MORTE DAR⸗
THUR WITH THE DOLOUROUS
DEATH AND DEPARTING
OUT OF THIS WORLD
OF THEM ALL.

Title Page.
From *Le Morte D'Arthur*.

17

The achieving of the Sangreal.

The Achieving of the Sangreal.
From *Le Morte D'Arthur.*

MERLIN TAKETH THE CHILD ARTHUR INTO HIS KEEPING

Merlin Taketh the Child Arthur into His Keeping.

19

Merlin. From
Le Morte D'Arthur.

THE LADY OF THE LAKE
TELLETH ARTHVR OF THE
SWORD EXCALIBVR

The Lady of the Lake
Telleth Arthur of the Sword Excalibur.

Vignette. From
Le Morte D'Arthur.

Vignette. From
Le Morte D'Arthur.

Vignette. From
Le Morte D'Arthur.

Merlin and Nimue.

ARTHVR AND
THE STRANGE
MANTLE

Arthur and the Strange Mantle.

HOW. FOVR. QVEENS. FOVND. LAVNCELOT. SLEEPING.

How Four Queens Found Launcelot Sleeping.

SIR. LAVNCELOT.
AND. THE. WITCH.
HELLAWES.

Sir Lancelot and the Witch Hellawes.

26

HOW LA BEALE
ISOVD NVRSED
SIR TRISTRAM

How La Beale Isoud Nursed Sir Tristram.

How Sir Tristram Drank of the Love Drink.

La Beale Isoud at Joyous Gard.   From *Le Morte D'Arthur.*

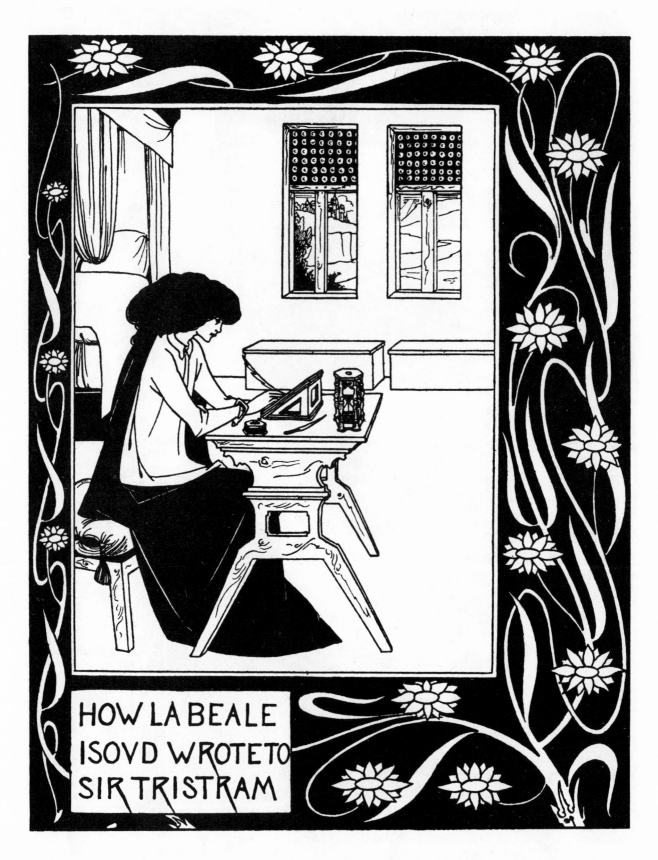

HOW LA BEALE
ISOVD WROTE TO
SIR TRISTRAM

How La Beale Isoud Wrote to Sir Tristram.

How King Marke Found Sir Tristram.

How Morgan Le Fay Gave a Shield to Sir Tristram.

How Sir Bedivere Cast the Sword Excalibur into the Water.

Vignette. From
Le Morte D'Arthur.

Vignette. From
Le Morte D'Arthur.

Vignette. From
Le Morte D'Arthur.

Vignette. From
Le Morte D'Arthur.

Vignette. From
Le Morte D'Arthur.

Vignette. From
Le Morte D'Arthur.

Vignette. From
Le Morte D'Arthur.

How King Mark and Sir Dinadan Heard Sir Palomides

Making Great Sorrow and Mourning for La Beale Isoud.

How Sir Launcelot Was Known

by Dame Elaine.

How a Devil in Woman's Likeness

Would Have Tempted Sir Bors.

41

How Queen Guenever

Rode on Maying.

How Queen Guenever Made Her a Nun.

"Of a Neophyte, and
How the Black Art Was Revealed Unto Him."

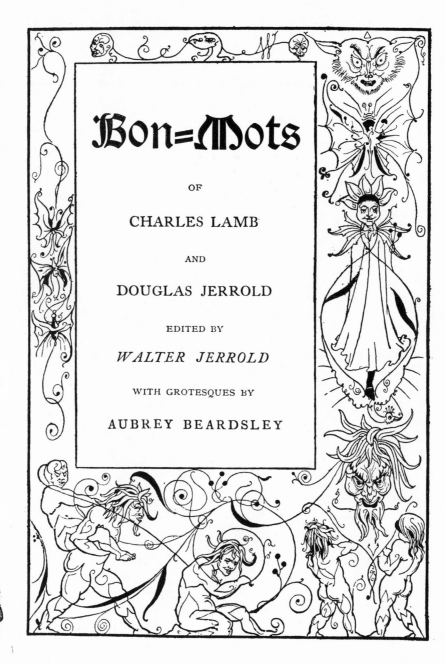

Title Page from *Bon-Mots*
of Charles Lamb
and Douglas Jerrold.

Frontispiece to *Bon-Mots*
of Charles Lamb
and Douglas Jerrold.

Chloe. From *Bon-Mots*
of Charles Lamb
and Douglas Jerrold.

A Grotesque.
From *Bon-Mots*
of Charles Lamb
and Douglas Jerrold.

Two Grotesques.
From *Bon-Mots*
of Charles Lamb
and Douglas Jerrold.

Monkey in Frock Coat.
From *Bon-Mots*
of Charles Lamb
and Douglas Jerrold.

A Satyr.
From *Bon-Mots
of Charles Lamb
and Douglas Jerrold.*

A Conversation.
From *Bon-Mots
of Charles Lamb
and Douglas Jerrold.*

A Drummer.
From *Bon-Mots
of Charles Lamb
and Douglas Jerrold.*

A Black Cat.
From *Bon-Mots
of Charles Lamb
and Douglas Jerrold.*

The Snare of Vintage.
From *Lucian's True History*.

Design. Intended for
Lucian's True History,
but not published.

The Pseudonym Library Poster.

Salome:
Cover Design.

Salome:
Supressed Title Page.

Salome:
Title Page Published.

Salome:
Contents Page Design.

Salome:
The Woman in the Moon.

Salome:
The Platonic Lament.

Salome:
The Peacock Skirt.

Salome:
John and Salome.

Salome:
Original of The Toilette of Salome.

Salome:
The Toilette of Salome, Published.

Salome:
Original of Enter Herodias.

Salome:
Enter Herodias, Published.

Salome:
The Eyes of Herod.

Salome:
The Stomach Dance.

Salome:
The Dancer's Reward.

Salome:
Salome with St. John's Head.

Salome:
The Climax.

Salome:
The Black Cape.

Salome:
Tailpiece.

Frontispiece to Plays by John Davidson.

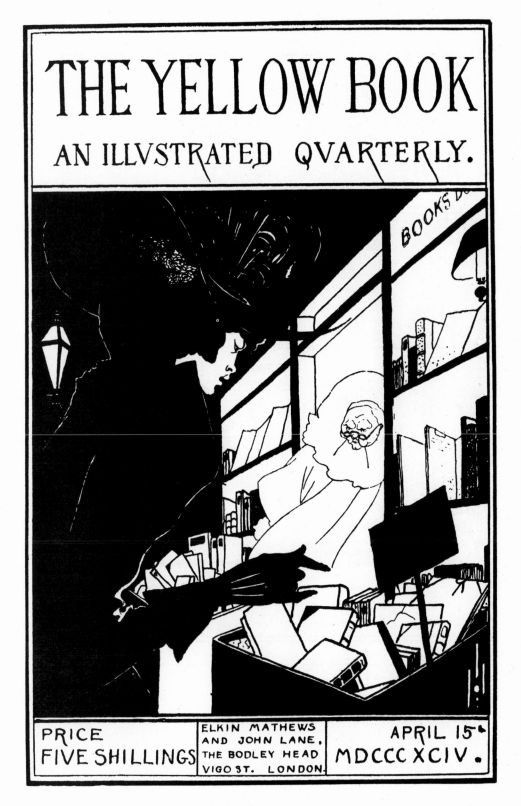

Design for Cover of *The Yellow Book* Prospectus.

Cover design for *The Yellow Book,* Volume I.

Portrait of Mrs. Patrick Campbell.
From *The Yellow Book*, Volume I.

Comedy-Ballet of Marionettes I.
From *The Yellow Book*, Volume II.

Comedy-Ballet of Marionettes II.
From *The Yellow Book,*
Volume II.

Comedy-Ballet of Marionettes III.
From *The Yellow Book,*
Volume II.

Garçons de Café.
From *The Yellow Book*, Volume II.

The Slippers of Cinderella.
From *The Yellow Book,* Volume II.

Cover Design. For *The Yellow Book,* Volume III.

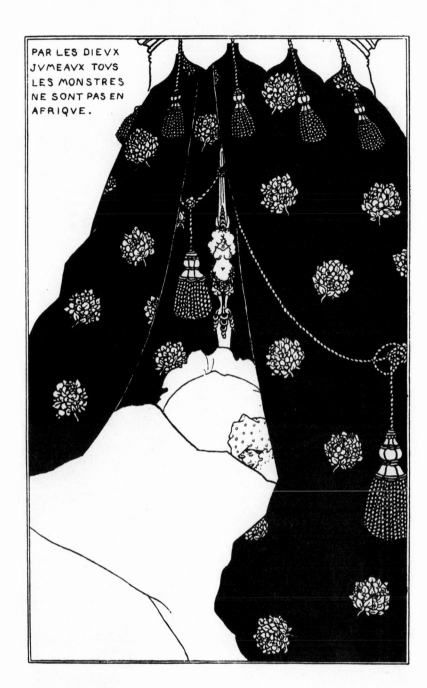

Title-Page Design.
From *The Yellow Book,*
Volume III.

Portrait of Himself.
From *The Yellow Book,*
Volume III.

Lady Gold's Escort. From *The Yellow Book*, Volume III.

The Wagnerites.
From *The Yellow Book*, Volume III.

La Dame aux Camelias,
From The Yellow Book, Volume III.

The Mysterious Rose Garden.
From *The Yellow Book*, Volume III.

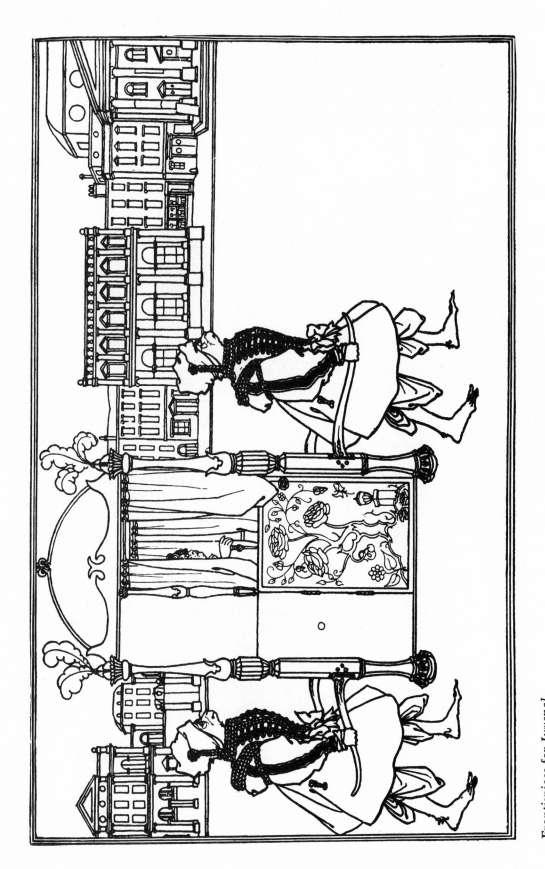

Frontispiece for *Juvenal*.
From *The Yellow Book*, Volume IV.

Design for *Yellow Book cover*. (Not used).

Madame Réjane.

VENUS.

Venus Between Terminal Gods.

The Return of Tannhäuser to the Venusberg.

Autumn.
From a Design for a Calendar.

A Child at Its Mother's Bed.
From *The Sketch*.

The Scarlet Pastorale. From *The Sketch*.

Isolde. From *The Studio*.

A Catalogue Cover.

Design for Frontispiece
of *Earl Lavender*.

Messalina.

93

Design for End-Paper of *Pierrot*.

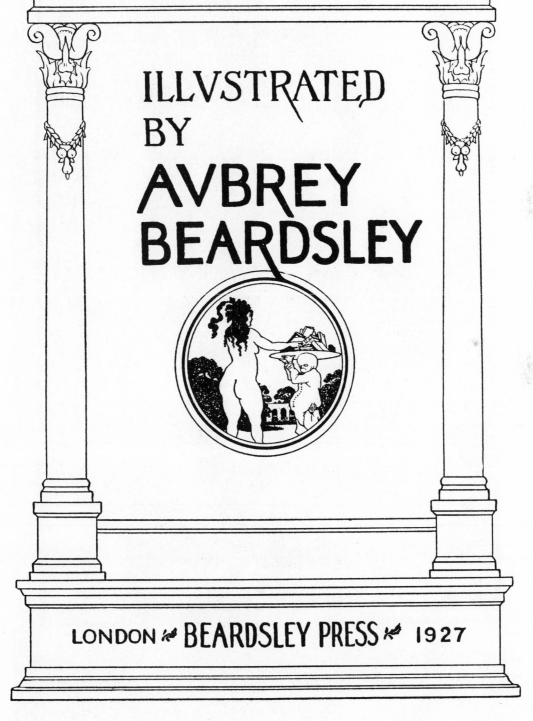

:ARISTOPHANES:
LYSISTRATA

ILLVSTRATED
BY
AVBREY
BEARDSLEY

LONDON · BEARDSLEY PRESS · 1927

Lysistrata: Frontispiece.

Lysistrata: Title Page.

Lysistrata: Lysistrata Haranguing the Athenian Women.

Lysistrata: Lysistrata Defending the Acropolis.

Lysistrata: Adoration of the Penis.

Lysistrata: Cinesias Soliciting Myrrhina.

Lysistrata: The Toilet of Lampito.

101

Lysistrata: Two Athenian Women in Distress.

Lysistrata: The Examination of the Herald.

Lysistrata: The Lacedemonian Ambassadors.

105   *The Rape of the Lock:* The Dream.

The Rape of the Lock: The Billet-Doux.

The Rape of the Lock: The Toilet.

The Rape of the Lock: The Baron's Prayer.

The Rape of the Lock: The Barge.

The Rape of the Lock: The Rape of the Lock.

The Rape of the Lock: The Cave of Spleen.

The Rape of the Lock: The Battle of the Beaux and the Belles.

The Rape of the Lock:
The New Star.

The Rape of the Lock:
Cover Design.

113

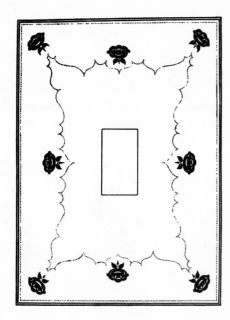

The Rape of the Lock:
Cover Design.
From the Bijou edition.

Prospectus of *The Savoy*.

Another Design
for the Prospectus of *The Savoy*.

Cover Design for *The Savoy*, No. 1

AUBREY
BEARDSLEY.
1896.

Title-Page. From *The Savoy,* Nos. 1 and 2.

The Three Musicians. From *The Savoy*, No. 1.

The Bathers. From *The Savoy,* No. 1.

The Abbé. From *The Savoy*, No. 1.

The Toilet of Helen. From *The Savoy*, No. 1.

A Large Christmas Card. From *The Savoy*, No. 1.

A Foot-note. From *The Savoy*, No. 2.

The Ecstasy of St. Rose of Lima.
From *The Savoy*, No. 2.

The Coiffing. From *The Savoy*, No. 3.

125

The Fourth Tableau of *Das Rheingold*.
From *The Savoy*, No. 6.

The Death of Pierrot. From *The Savoy*, No. 6.

Ave Atque Vale.
From *The Savoy*, No. 7.

Don Juan, Sganarelle and the Beggar.
From *The Savoy*, No. 8.

MRS PINCHWIFE

Mrs. Margery Pinchwife.
From *The Savoy*, No. 8.

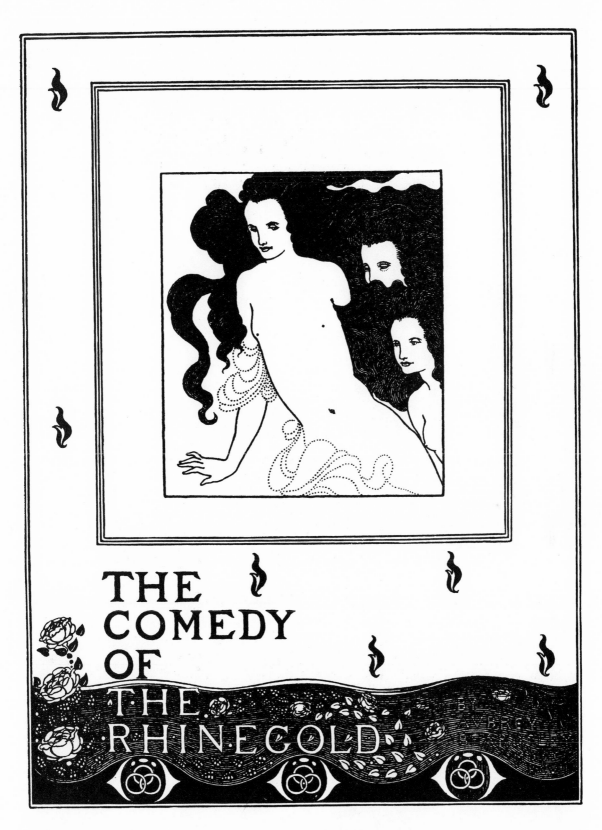

Frontispiece to the Comedy of *Das Rheingold*.
From *The Savoy*, No. 8.

Erda. To Illustrate
Das Rheingold.
From *The Savoy*, No. 8.

Alberich. To Illustrate
Das Rheingold.
From *The Savoy*, No. 8.

Count Valmont. From *Les Liaisons Dangereuses.*
From *The Savoy*, No. 8.

Et in Arcadia Ego. From *The Savoy*, No. 8.

Apollo Pursues Daphne.

Design for Wrapper of Catalogue of Rare Books, No. 7.

Frontispiece to *The Pierrot of the Minute.*

Frontispiece
to *A Book of Bargains.*

Cul-de-Lampe
to *The Pierrot of the Minute.*

138

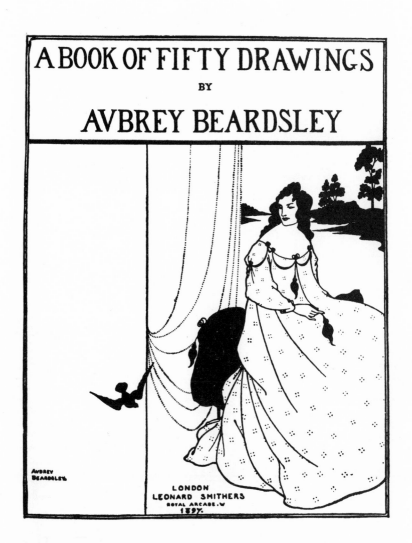

Cover Design.
From *A Book of Fifty Drawings.*

Book-Plate of the Artist.

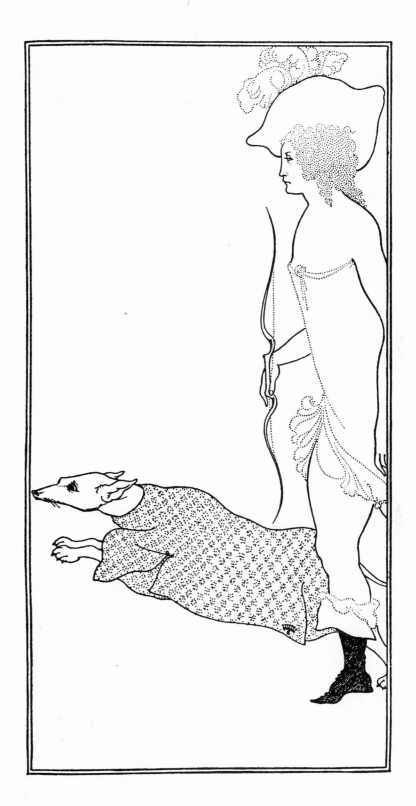

Atalanta in Calydon.

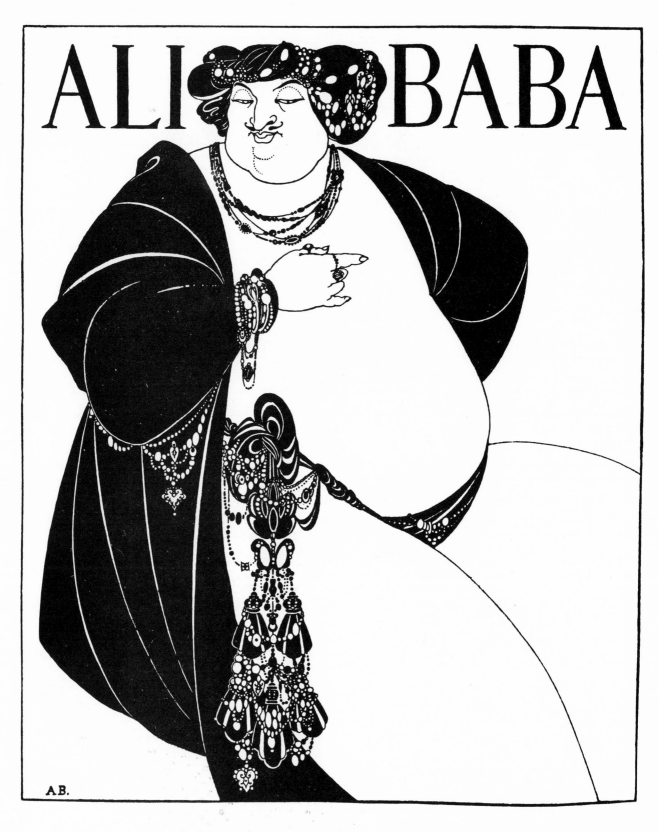

Ali Baba. Cover Design for the *Forty Thieves*.

Messalina Returning from the Bath.

143

D'Albert in Search of Ideals.
From *Mademoiselle de Maupin*.

The Lady at the Dressing Table.
From *Mademoiselle de Maupin*.

The Lady with the Rose.
From *Mademoiselle de Maupin*.

Cover Design to *Volpone* by Ben Jonson.

Frontispiece to *Volpone* by Ben Jonson.

Initial Letter S (Vulture) to *Volpone*.

Initial Letter V (Satyr) to *Volpone*.

Initial Letter M (Venus) to *Volpone*.

Initial Letter V (Column) to *Volpone*.

Initial Letter V (Elephant) to *Volpone*.

A FOREWORD TO THE DRAWINGS REPRODUCED FROM FIFTY DRAWINGS BY AUBREY BEARDSLEY, SELECTED FROM THE COLLECTION OF MR. H. S. NICHOLS

AUBREY BEARDSLEY's style and subject matter were not only widely imitated, but many imitations went so far as to constitute forgery. One of the earliest known cases of forged work emanated from the workshop of Beardsley's own publisher and supposed friend, Leonard Smithers. Another notorious forgery, according to the great Beardsley scholars of today, consisted of the drawings on the following pages. However, the art critics of this century's second decade appeared to be less astute. The September, 1919 issue of *Vanity Fair* included an article entitled "Aubrey Beardsley: Vintage of 1919....A New Picture Game for Tired Critics" by Oliver Brenning, in which the Nichols collection is discussed.

"...As it was generally known that practically all of Beardsley's drawings had been carefully recorded, and often reproduced, the announcement made last Spring of an exhibition in New York in April of about eighty hitherto unkown examples of Beardsley's work made no little stir in art circles. As the announcement ran, they were to come as a 'complete and startling surprise.' To students of Beardsley's work, however, they were not a surprise at all, they turned out to be exactly what was expected. Three of New York's great dailies notwithstanding appeared with glowing accounts of the exhibition, stating that these drawings were magnificent specimens of Beardsley's art. It was at this point that Mr. A. E. Gallatin, who is an authority on Beardsley...boldly went right ahead and attacked these eighty alleged drawings without quarter. All of his cohorts agreed that the drawings were not only not by Beardsley but that they were an insult to the artist's memory. Chief among their weak points, aside from their faulty technique was the fact that they were twice as large as any known examples, that they were drawn on cardboard, which Beardsley never used, and finally—probably the most telling feature of all—that they were not included in Aymar Vallance's iconography which was revised by Aubrey Beardsley himself.

"This controversy raged in the columns of several metropolitan, as well as provincial newspapers. It became the most widely discussed incident in the art world of recent years. In fact, one wondered if the American public did not take a far greater interest in artistic matters than it has been generally credited with, after all....It is hardly necessary to say that no artist would make a design by taking parts of four previously executed drawings, making very bad copies of them and throwing them together without any regard whatever for design or composition.

"I am afraid that the art writers on the New York papers will not find their remarks taken very seriously next winter—that is if the public is not quick to forget that they swallowed the Great Beardsley Hoax without a murmur."

We have, nevertheless, included the Nichols drawings as a matter of curiosity and for the enlightenment of the Beardsley collector. A study of the forgeries might help avoid a costly mistake. One becomes even more convinced of Beardsley's unique genius and his ability to capture excitement and beauty with lines when one recognizes the failures that the forger's attempts produced.   —B.S.H.

Toilette of a Courtezan.

Remorse.

A Messalina.

The Jilted Pierrot.

Peacock and Rising Sun.

The Inquisitive Nun.

Pan and the Wood-Nymphs.

AUBREY BEARDSLEY

Cover Design for a Journal of Fashion.

Portrait of a Lady.

Lady Combing Her Hair.

Oscar Wilde.

Masked Danseuse.

165

AUBREY BEARDSLEY

The Twins.

Design for *The Savoy*.

Design for a Book-cover.

Aubrey Beardsley.

169

After the Bath.

Lady in Rose Pattern Dress.

J. McNeill Whistler.

AUBREY BEARDSLEY.

173

J. McNeill Whistler.

Lady and Powder-puff.

Design for a Theatre Poster.

The Crinoline Skirt.

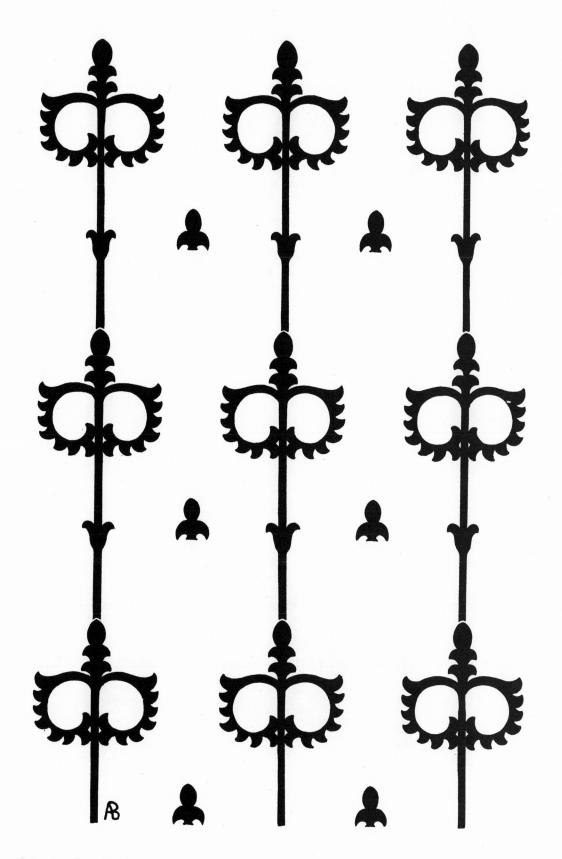

Design for a Book-cover.

A Nude Woman Poised
on a Wave Arranging Her Hair.

Belinda's Toilet.

179

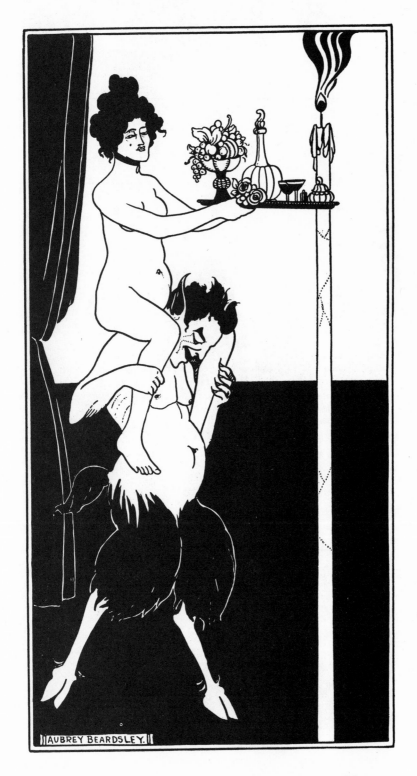

Satyr Carrying a Woman.

The Finishing Touch.

The Dreamer.

An Artist's Model.

Cover Design.

The Pestilence.

AUBREY BEARDSLEY

Oriental Dancer.

Design for a Theatre Poster.

Dancing to Pan's Pipes.

187

My Hostess.

Lady with Doves.

189

The Black Domino.

Old Age and Youth.

A Masquerader.

193   **Womanly Beauty.**

Design for an en tête.

Aubrey Beardsley.

194

The Satyr-Coiffeur and the Lady.

Blowing Bubbles.

A Book-cover Design.

197

Design for a Church Window.

LIST OF DRAWINGS BY AUBREY BEARDSLEY

Items preceded by asterisk indicate illustrations in the present book.
Figure numbers, however, do not correspond.

JUVENILIA

1. A CARNIVAL. Long procession of many figures in fifteenth and sixteenth century costume. Water-colour drawing. Unpublished. Given by the artist to his grandfather, the late Surgeon-Major William Pitt. *c.* 1880.

2. THE JACKDAW OF RHEIMS, set of illustrations to the poem. Unpublished. *c.* 1884.

3. VIRGIL'S "ÆNEID," nine comic illustrations to Book II. The title-page, written in rough imitation of printing, with the Artist's naïf and inaccurate spelling, is as follows:—ILLUSTRATIONES DE | LIBER SECUNDUS | ÆNEIDOS | PUBLIUS WIRGIUS MARONIS | by | Beardslius | de | Brightelmstoniensis. The illustrations are entitled:—
   I. Laocoon hurleth his spear against the horse.
   II. Laocoon and son crunched up.
   III. Little July tries to keep up with Papa. Old Father Anchises sitteth on Papa's shoulders and keeps a good look-out.
   IV. Parvi Iulus.
   V. Helen.
   VI. Panthus departs, bag and baggage.
   VII. Sinon telleth his tale unto King Priam.
   VIII. One of the cinders of Illium.
   IX. (No title.) The drawing, to illustrate two comic verses written at the top of the paper, represents Æneas being carried up into the air by means of a balloon attached to his helmet.
   All the above are drawn in ordinary ink upon plain white paper of the kind used for rough work at the school, and all are of uniform size, 7¼ × 5 inches, except No. 9, which is on a double-size sheet, measuring 7¼ × 10 inches. Unpublished. (Property of H. A. Payne, Esq.) September to December 1886.

4. VIRGIL'S "ÆNEID," nineteen humorous sketches illustrative of Book II., entitled:—
   I. Æneas relateth the tale to Dido.
   II. Laocoon hurls the spear.
   III. Sinon is brought before Priam.
   IV. Calchas will not betray anyone.
   *V. "All night I lay hid in a weedy lake."
   *VI. The Palladium is snatched away.
   *VII. The Palladium jumpeth.
   *VIII. Laocoon sacrificeth on the sand.
   IX. Sinon opens the bolt.
   X. Hector's ghost.
   *XI. Æneas heareth the clash of arms.
   XII. Panthus fleeth.
   XIII. Pyrrhus exulteth.
   *XIV. Death of Priam.
   *XV. Æneas debateth whether he shall slay Helen.
   *XVI. Venus appeareth to Æneas.
   *XVII. Jupiter hurls the lightning.
   *XVIII. Æneas and company set out from Troy.
   XIX. Æneas seeth Creusa's ghost.

The above drawings in ordinary ink are contained in a copy-book, 8 × 6½ inches. Unpublished. Exhibited in London at Carfax & Co.'s Galleries, October 1904. (Property of Harold Hartley, Esq.) End of 1886.

5. THE POPE WEIGHS HEAVILY ON THE CHURCH. Pen-drawing contained in the same copy-book with the last-named.

6. JOHN SMILES, a comic illustration to the school history book, representing King John in the act of signing Magna Charta. Pen-drawing on paper 7¼ × 5 inches. Unpublished. (Property of H. A. Payne, Esq.)

7. SAINT BRADLAUGH, M.P., a caricature. Pen-drawing on a half sheet of notepaper. Unpublished. (Property of H. A. Payne, Esq.)

8. AUTUMN TINTS. Caricature in black and white of the artist's schoolmaster, Mr Marshall, expounding to his pupils the beauties of nature. Unpublished. Given to Ernest Lambert, Esq., Brighton. *c.* 1886-7.
   Beside the above-named there must have been numbers of such drawings belonging to this early period; for in his schooldays Aubrey Beardsley was, to quote the words of Mr H. A. Payne, "constantly doing these little, rough, humorous sketches, which he gave away wholesale." Many have been destroyed or lost, others dispersed abroad. Thus, for instance, one old Brighton Grammar School boy, C. E. Pitt-Schenkel, told Mr Payne that he was in possession of some, which he took out to South Africa.

9. THE JUBILEE CRICKET ANALYSIS. Eleven tiny pen-and-ink sketches, entitled respectively:—
   I. A good bowler.
   II. Over.
   III. Slip.
   IV. Square leg.
   V. Shooters.
   VI. Caught.
   VII. A block.
   VIII. A demon bowler.
   IX. Stumped.
   X. Long leg.
   XI. Cutting a ball.
All these subjects being represented, in humorous fashion, by literal equivalents. These drawings, though they cannot pretend to any merit, are notable as the earliest specimens to be published of the artist's work. Together they formed a whole-page photo-lithographic illustration in *Past and Present*, the Brighton Grammar School Magazine, June 1887.

10. CONGREVE'S "DOUBLE DEALER," illustration of a scene from, comprising Maskwell and Lady Touchwood. Pen drawing with sepia wash, on a sheet of paper 13½ × 11

inches. Unpublished. (Property of H. A. Payne, Esq.) Signed and dated June 30, 1888.

11. HOLYWELL STREET. Wash drawing. First published in *The Poster*, Aug. - Sept. 1898. Republished in "The Early Work of Aubrey Beardsley, with a Prefatory Note by H. C. Marillier." John Lane, March 1899. (Property of Charles B. Cochran, Esq., 1888.)

12. THE PAY OF THE PIED PIPER: A LEGEND OF HAMELIN TOWN. Eleven line drawings in illustration of, as follows :—

   I. Entrance of Councillors, headed by Beadle carrying a mace. Reproduced in *The Westminster Budget*, March 25, 1898.

   II. Rats feeding upon a cheese in a dish. Reproduced in *Westminster Budget*, March 25, 1898.

   III. Child climbing into an armchair to escape from the rats. Reproduced in *The Poster*, Aug.-Sept. 1898.

   IV. The Sitting of the Council, under the presidency of the Burgomaster.

   V. Deputation of Ladies.

   VI. Two rats on their hind legs, carrying off the Beadle's mace : behind them are three rats running. Reproduced in *Westminster Budget*, March 25, 1898.

   VII. Meeting between the Beadle and the Piper.

   VIII. The rats follow the Piper out of the town. Republished in *Westminster Budget*, March 25, 1898, and in *The Poster*, Aug.-Sept. 1898.

   IX. Citizens rejoice at the departure of the rats.

   X. The Piper is dismissed by the Beadle. Republished in *Westminster Budget*, March 25, 1898, and also in *Magazine of Art*, May 1898.

   XI. The Piper entices away the children.

The above illustrations vary in size from $3\frac{1}{4} \times 2\frac{1}{2}$ to $6\frac{1}{2} \times 4\frac{1}{2}$ inches. They are unsigned, but a prefatory note describes them as being "the perfectly original designs and drawings of a boy now in the school, A. V. Beardsley"; and adds: "Our regret is that, lacking experience in the preparation of drawings for the photo-engraver, the reproductions should fall so far short of the original sketches." Published in the programme and book of words of the Brighton Grammar School Annual Entertainment at the Dome, on Wednesday, Dec. 19, 1888; bound up afterwards with *Past and Present*, February 1889. Latter part of 1888.

13. A SCRAP-BOOK, size $9\frac{1}{2} \times 7$ inches, the fly-leaf inscribed, in his own writing, *A. Beardsley*, 6/5/90, presented by the artist's mother to Robert Ross, Esq. Contains the following drawings, mounted as scraps :—

   *I. Manon Lescaut, three drawings to illustrate different scenes from. Executed with very fine pen and ink, the latter having, as compared with maturer works, a brownish tinge. One of them first appeared in " A Second Book of Fifty Drawings

by Aubrey Beardsley" (Leonard Smithers, December 1898), and all three were included in "The Later Work of Aubrey Beardsley" (John Lane, 1901).

   II. La Dame aux Camélias. $4\frac{3}{8}$ inches square, pen and brownish ink with wash. First published in "Second Book," and afterwards in "Later Work." This is a totally different design from that which afterwards appeared, with the same title, in "The Yellow Book." See below.

   III. Tartarin, two illustrations of, in pencil and colours, size $4\frac{1}{8} \times 2\frac{3}{4}$ and $4\frac{1}{2} \times 3\frac{1}{2}$ inches respectively.

   IV. La Leçon (Madame Bovary). $5\frac{1}{4} \times 6\frac{3}{4}$. Chinese white and dark sepia wash. First published in "Second Book," and again in "Later Work."

   V. L'Abbé Birotteau (Curé de Tours). 3×2 inches. Pen-and-ink with wash, on pale greenish paper.

   VI. L'Abbé Troubert (Curé de Tours). $5 \times 2\frac{3}{4}$ inches. Dark sepia wash.

   VII. Madame Bovary. $5\frac{5}{8} \times 3\frac{1}{8}$ inches. Pencil. First published in "Second Book," and again in "Later Work."

   VIII. Sapho (Daudet). Wanting. Over its place has been gummed another drawing, also wanting, its title written at the foot, *L'homme qui rit*.

   IX. Le Cousin Pons. $5\frac{1}{8} \times 2\frac{3}{8}$ inches. Indian ink.

   X. Portrait of Alphonse Daudet. $2\frac{3}{4} \times 2\frac{3}{16}$ inches. Indian ink on pale blue paper.

   XI. Watteau, Ma Cousine (Cousin Pons). $5\frac{1}{2} \times 2\frac{3}{4}$ inches. Pen-and-ink with wash on pale grey toned paper.

   XII. Mademoiselle Gamard (Curé de Tours). $3\frac{1}{8} \times 2\frac{1}{8}$ inches. Indian ink wash.

   XIII. Madame Cibot (Cousin Pons). $4 \times 2\frac{7}{8}$ inches. Indian ink wash.

   XIV. (Jack) Attendons ! $3\frac{5}{8}$ inches high, irregular silhouette. Dark sepia wash.

   XV. Jeanne D'Arc, the childhood of. $9 \times 3\frac{3}{8}$ inches. Sepia and madder wash on toned paper. First published in "Second Book," again in "Later Work."

   *XVI. Frontispiece to Balzac's "Contes Drôlatiques." $6\frac{3}{4} \times 4\frac{1}{8}$ inches. Drawn after the manner of Richard Doyle. First published in "Second Book," again in "Later Work."

   XVII. Phèdre (Act ii. scene 5). $3\frac{7}{8} \times 3\frac{1}{2}$ inches. Pencil and colours. First published in "Second Book," again in "Later Work."

   XVIII. Manon Lescaut, three-quarter length, woman to left, with fan. $5\frac{1}{4} \times 3\frac{1}{2}$ inches. Water-colour on grey paper. First published in "Second Book," again in "Later Work."

   XIX. Beatrice Cenci. $6\frac{1}{8} \times 2\frac{3}{4}$ inches. Pencil and sepia wash. First published in "Second Book," again in "Later Work."

Unless otherwise stated as above, the works in this collection are unpublished ; all were executed 1889-90.

LATER WORK.

*14. FRANCESCA DI RIMINI (Dante). Head in profile, to left; pencil. First published in "Later Work."

15. DANTE AT THE COURT OF CAN GRANDE DELLA SCALA. Circular design, in pencil. (Property of Miss H. Glover.)

16. DANTE IN EXILE. Dante seated on the left, the words of the Sonnet inscribed on the right, with decorations recalling some design of William Blake's. Signed A.V.B. First published in "Later Work." (Formerly the property of the late Hampden Gurney, Esq.)

17. "I SAW THREE SHIPS COME SAILING BY ON CHRISTMAS DAY IN THE MORNING." Pencil. Designed as a Christmas card for the late Rev. Alfred Gurney. Published in "Later Work." c. 1890-1.

*18. HAIL MARY. Profile of a head to left. Pencil drawing, $4\frac{1}{2} \times 5\frac{1}{4}$ inches. First published in The Studio, May 1898, again in "Early Work." (Property of Frederick H. Evans, Esq.) 1891.

19. HEAD, three-quarter face to right, with a Wreath of Grapes and Vine Leaves and background of tree trunks. Lead-pencil sketch $5\frac{1}{2} \times 5\frac{5}{8}$ inches. Unpublished. (Property of John Lane, Esq.) circa 1891.

20. THEL GATHERING THE LILY. Pen-and-ink with water-colour wash. (Formerly the property of Robert Ross, Esq.)

21. TWO FIGURES IN A GARRET, both seated, a woman haranguing a young man. Ink and wash sketch, $3\frac{1}{4} \times 4\frac{1}{8}$ inches. Published in "Early Work." (Property of Frederick H. Evans, Esq.)

22. E. BURNE-JONES. Portrait sketch in pen-and-ink, with slight wash. A memorandum of Aubrey Beardsley's first call on Sir Edward Burne-Jones, dated Sunday, 12th July 1891, and signed with monogram, A.V.B. Size, $6\frac{3}{4} \times 4\frac{1}{8}$ inches. Eight copies only. Printed on India paper. Published by James Tregaskis, Caxton Head, High Holborn, in 1899. July 1891.

23. THE WITCH OF ATLAS. Pen-and-ink and water-colour wash. First reproduced (lacking ornamental border) in "Second Book," again in "Later Work." (Formerly the property of Robert Ross, Esq.)

24. MOLIÈRE. Blue water-colour wash. First published in "Later Work." (Formerly the property of Robert Ross, Esq.)

*25. DIE GÖTTERDÄMMERUNG. Decorative composition in white and Indian ink, influenced by Burne-Jones. First published in "Second Book," again in "Later Work." (Formerly the property of Robert Ross, Esq.)

*26. SOLEIL COUCHANT. Decorative composition in Indian ink. (The motif of the central part was subsequently adapted for a vignette in the "Morte Darthur," Book II. chap. xii.) First published in "Later Work." (Formerly the property of the late Hampden Gurney, Esq.)

27. TANNHÄUSER. Study for decorative composition, in Indian ink. $5\frac{5}{8} \times 7\frac{1}{2}$ inches. First published in "Later Work." (Property of Dr Rowland Thurnam.) 1891.

*28. WITHERED SPRING. Decorative composition in Indian ink. Catalogued in "Fifty Drawings" as "Lament of the Dying Year." (The motif of the central part was subsequently adapted for a vignette in the "Morte Darthur," Book I. chap. xii.) First published in "Later Work." (Property of Dr Rowland Thurnam.)

29. I. PERSEUS. Pen-and-ink and light wash. Design for an upright panel, with standing nude figure, above it a frieze of smaller figures. $18 \times 6\frac{3}{4}$ inches. First published in "Early Work." (Property of Frederick H. Evans, Esq.)

II. A pencil sketch of two figures, unfinished, on the reverse of the preceding. Published in "Early Work."

30. L'ABBÉ MOURET. Decorative design for frontispiece of Zola's "La Faute de l'Abbé Mouret." Ink and wash. First published in "Under the Hill." John Lane. 1904. (Property of John Lane, Esq.)

*31. HAMLET PATRIS MANEM SEQUITUR. Pencil drawing. Printed in red, as frontispiece to The Bee, the Magazine of the Blackburn Technical School, November 1891; reprinted, in black, in "Second Book," again in "Early Work." Latter part 1891.

32. PERSEUS AND THE MONSTRE. Pencil design, $5\frac{1}{2} \times 7\frac{1}{2}$ inches. First appeared in illustration of an article entitled, "The Invention of Aubrey Beardsley," by Aymer Vallance, in The Magazine of Art, May 1898; again in "Early Work." (Property of Aymer Vallance, Esq.) 1891.

33. THE PROCESSION OF JEANNE D'ARC. Pencil outline, treatment inspired by Mantegna, $19\frac{1}{2}$ long by $6\frac{1}{2}$ inches high. First published in Magazine of Art, May 1898; again as double page in "Second Book"; again, reduced, in collotype, in "Early Work." (Property of Frederick H. Evans, Esq.) 1891-2.

A pen-and-ink version of the Procession, 30 inches long by 7 high, was made subsequently, about the Spring of 1892, for Robert Ross, Esq. Published in The Studio; see below.

*34. THE LITANY OF MARY MAGDALEN. Pencil drawing. First published in "Second Book," again in "Later Work." (Formerly Property of More Adey, Esq.) 1892.

35. THE VIRGIN AND LILY. Madonna standing in front of a Renaissance niche and surrounded by Saints, among them St John Baptist kneeling. Pencil outline. Reproduced in photogravure in "Later Work."

(Formerly the property of the late Rev. Alfred Gurney, afterwards in the possession of his son, the late Hampden Gurney, Esq.)

36. CHILDREN DECORATING A TERMINAL GOD. Pen-and-ink. (Formerly the property of M. Puvis de Chavannes.)

37. FRED BROWN, N.E.A.C. Pen-and-ink sketch of the art-master in studio. Signed with monogram A.V.B. First published in "Under the Hill." (Property of Miss Nellie Syrett.)

38. STUDY OF FIGURES, horizontal fragment from, containing five heads and parts of two more. Pencil. Published in "Under the Hill." (Property of Miss Nellie Syrett.)

*39. PORTRAIT OF THE ARTIST. Full face. Pen-and-ink. First published in "Second Book," again in "Later Work." (Presented by Robert Ross, Esq., to the British Museum.)

40. SIDONIA THE SORCERESS. A design to illustrate Meinhold's Romance, representing Sidonia, not in religious habit, with the demon-cat, Chim. William Morris's criticism that the face of Sidonia was not pretty enough, and another suggested improvement on the part of a friend of Aubrey Beardsley's, induced him to try to better the picture by altering the hair. The result was so far from satisfactory that it is almost certain that the drawing was destroyed by the artist. First half of 1892.

41. LE DÉBRIS D'UN POETE. Pen-and-ink. First published in "Aubrey Beardsley," by Arthur Symons (Sign of the Unicorn, London, 1898). (Property of André Raffalovich, Esq.)

42. INCIPIT VITA NOVA. Chinese, white, and Indian ink on brown paper. First published in "Second Book," again in "Later Work." (Property of Messrs Carfax & Co.) 1892.

43. HEAD OF AN ANGEL, in profile, to left, flaming heart held in left hand. Pencil, on a half-sheet of grey notepaper, signed with monogram A.V.B. $5\frac{3}{4} \times 3\frac{7}{8}$ inches. First published in photogravure "Second Book," again in "Later Work"; also printed in 4-inch square form on card for private distribution, Christmas 1905. (Property of the artist's sister, Mrs George Bealby Wright [Miss Mabel Beardsley].) c. 1892.

44. ADORAMUS TE. Four angels in a circle (7 inches in diameter) playing musical instruments, pencil and coloured chalks. Signed A.V.B. monogram. Designed as a Christmas card for the late Rev. Alfred Gurney. First published in photogravure in "Second Book," again in "Later Work." (Property of Mrs George Bealby Wright.)

45. A CHRISTMAS CAROL. Two angels, one of them playing a hand-organ, in a circle ($7\frac{3}{4}$ inches diameter), pencil and coloured chalks. Designed as a Christmas card for the late Rev. Alfred Gurney. First published in photogravure in "Second Book," again in "Later Work." Also in photogravure, 3 inches diameter, for private circulation. (Property of Mrs George Bealby Wright.) Christmas, 1892.

46. LA FEMME INCOMPRISE. Pen-and-ink and wash. First published in the spring number of To-Day, 1895; again in the Idler magazine, March 1897.

*47. SANDRO BOTTICELLI, three-quarter face to left, pencil, signed with monogram A.V.B.; $14 \times 7\frac{3}{4}$ inches; a reconstruction of the Florentine painter's physiognomy from his extant works, to illustrate Aubrey Beardsley's theory that every artist tends to reproduce his own physical type. Presented by the artist to Aymer Vallance, Esq. First published in the Magazine of Art, May 1898; afterwards in "Early Work." c. 1892-3.

48. RAPHAEL SANZIO. Full-length figure, three-quarter face to left, a decorative panel in pen-and-ink, $10\frac{3}{4} \times 3\frac{7}{8}$ inches, exclusive of border lines. Unpublished. (Property of Messrs Obach & Co.)

49. CEPHALUS AND PROCRIS. Pen-and-ink.

*50. SMALL BOOKMARKER, woman undressing, a Turkish table in the foreground. Pen-and-ink. First published in "Second Book," again in "Later Work." (Property of Sir William Geary, Bart.) 1893.

51. HERMAPHRODITUS, seated figure, pencil and pale colour tints. Reproduced in colour in "Later Work." (Property of Julian Sampson, Esq.)

52. L'APRÈS-MIDI D'UN FAUNE, par Mallarmé; four designs extra-illustrating a copy of. One of them, a pen-and-ink vignette of a faun, full face, signed with monogram A.V.B., was published in "Second Book." The others unpublished. 1893.

53. DECORATIVE SKETCH DESIGN OF A SAILING SHIP. $1\frac{7}{8} \times 2\frac{1}{2}$ inches. Pen-and-ink on white from the back of a letter to Aymer Vallance, Esq. First published in Magazine of Art, May 1898; again in "Early Work." c. 1893.

54. ANGEL PLAYING HAND-ORGAN. Pen-and-ink and slight wash, on pale grey notepaper, from a letter to Aymer Vallance, Esq. First published in Magazine of Art, May 1898; again in "Early Work." c. 1893.

55. THE PALL MALL BUDGET, 1893 and 1894.
   I. MR H. A. JONES AND HIS BAUBLE; pen-and-ink. Feb. 2, 1893, p. 150.
   II. THE NEW COINAGE. Four designs that were not sent in for competition, p. 154. Another design, embodying a caricature of Queen Victoria, was suppressed.
   III. "BECKET" AT THE LYCEUM.
      1. Mr Irving as Becket; wash drawing. Feb. 9th, front page.
      2. Master Leo, p. 188.
      3. Queen Eleanor, p. 188.
      4. Margery, p. 188.
      5. The King makes a Move on the Board, p. 188.
      6. Miss Terry (as Rosamond), p. 188.
      7. Mr Gordon Craig, p. 190.

8. The Composer, p. 190.

IV. 1. THE DISAPPOINTMENT OF EMILE ZOLA, p. 202.
   2. EMILE ZOLA; a portrait, p. 204.
   (Republished in " Pall Mall Pictures of the
   Year," 1893, and in *The Studio*, June 1893.)

V. VERDI'S " FALSTAFF," AT MILAN, Feb. 16th.
   Initial letter V ; pen-and-ink, p. 236.
   Portrait of Verdi ; ink and wash, p. 236.

VI. POPE LEO XIII.'s JUBILEE, Feb. 23rd.
   The Pilgrim (old style), p. 270.
   The Pilgrim (new style), p. 270.

VII. THE REAPPEARANCE OF MRS BANCROFT.
   1. Mr Arthur Cecil (Baron Stein), p. 281.
   2. Mrs Bancroft (Lady Fairfax), p. 281.
   3. Mr Forbes Robertson (Julian Beauclere),p.281.
   4. Mr Bancroft (Count Orloff), p. 281.

VIII. CARICATURE OF A GOLF PLAYER, in classical helmet,
   March 9th, p. 376.

IX. ORPHEUS AT THE LYCEUM, March 16th.
   1. One of the Spirits, Act II., p. 395.
   2. Orpheus (Miss Clara Butt), p. 395.
   3. A Visitor at the Rehearsal, p. 395.
   4. Some Dresses in the Chorus, p. 395.

X. PORTRAIT OF THE LATE JULES FERRY : wash drawing, March 23rd, p. 435.

XI. BULLET-PROOF UNIFORM : Tommy Atkins thinks
   it rather fun, March 30, p. 491.

XII. MR FREDERICK HARRISON'S " IDEAL NOVELIST,"
   April 20, p. 620.

XIII. A NEW YEAR'S DREAM, after studying Mr Pennell's
   " Devils of Notre Dame." Republished in
   " Early Work." Jan. 4th, 1894, p. 8.

56. MR PARNELL, sketch portrait of the Irish party leader,
head and shoulders, three quarters face to left, pencil,
half tone reproduction, $4\frac{3}{4} \times 3\frac{1}{2}$ inches.

57. I. THE STUDIO. Design for wrapper in two states, the
original design containing a seated figure of Pan,
omitted in the later version. First state on brown
paper. The same, reduced, in black on green, for
prospectus, republished in *The Studio*, May 1898, and
again in " Early Work."

Second state, black on green, also in gold on rough
white paper for presentation to Royalty (Nov. 15th,
1893). The same, reduced, and printed in dark
green on white, for a prospectus, republished in " Early
Work." The same, enlarged and printed in black
on light green, for a poster.

THE STUDIO, No. 1, April 1893, accompanying an
article entitled " A New Illustrator : Aubrey Beardsley,"
by Joseph Pennell, contained :—

   II. Reduced reproduction of the pen-and-ink replica
   of Jeanne d'Arc procession. Republished as
   large folding supplement in No. 2.

*III. Siegfried, Act II., from the original drawing in line
   and wash, signed A.V.B., presented by the artist
   to Sir Edward Burne-Jones, after whose death
   it was given back by Lady Burne-Jones, to the

artist's mother, Mrs Beardsley. Republished
in " Early Work."

IV. The Birthday of Madame Cigale, line and wash,
   15 inches long by $9\frac{1}{2}$ inches high, influenced
   by Japanese models. Reproduced in " Early
   Work." (Property of Charles Holme, Esq.)

V. Les Revenants de Musique, line and wash. Reproduced in " Early Work." (Property of
   Charles Holme, Esq.)

VI. Salome with the head of St John the Baptist. Upright panel in Chinese ink on white, $10\frac{1}{8}$ by $5\frac{1}{8}$
   inches, exclusive of framing lines. This was the
   first design suggested to the artist by Oscar
   Wilde's French play of " Salome." It differs
   from the later version of the same subject in being
   richer and more complex. It contains the legend,
   omitted in the later version, *j'ai baisé ta bouche
   Iokanaan, j'ai baisé ta bouche*. The treatment is
   obviously influenced by Japanese work, and also
   by that of the French Symboliste school,
   e.g. Carlos Schwabe. Republished in " Early
   Work." Subsequently to its appearance in *The
   Studio*, the artist experimentally tinted it with
   green colour washes. In its final state it has
   not been published. (Formerly the property of
   Mrs Ernest Leverson, now of Miss K. Doulton.)

VII. Reduced reproduction of the second version of the
   Jeanne d'Arc procession. The same appeared,
   full size, as a folding plate supplement, in No.
   2 of *The Studio*, May 1893.

   In the first number of *The Studio* (April) also
   were published, by anticipation, four designs from
   the " Morte Darthur," due to begin its serial
   appearance in the following June, viz. :—

VIII. Initial letter I.

IX. Merlin taketh the child Arthur into his keeping
   (full page, including border).

X. Ornamental border for full page.

XI. Frieze for chapter-heading ; six men fighting,
   on foot, three of them panoplied. Reproduced
   in *Magazine of Art*, November 1896, " Fifty
   Drawings," *Idler*, March 1897, and *St Paul's*,
   April 9th, 1898. The original drawing is $13\frac{3}{4}$
   inches long by $4\frac{1}{2}$ inches. As may be seen,
   even in the reduced reproduction, one inch at
   either end was added by the artist at the request
   of his publisher, so as to increase the proportionate
   length of the ornament. Subsequently Mr
   Frederick H. Evans photographed the drawing,
   full size, and produced fifteen platinotype copies,
   of which twelve only were for sale, and the
   plate destroyed.

58. DESIGN OF DANDELIONS, for publishers' trade mark for
Dent & Co.

59. LE MORTE DARTHUR, by Sir Thomas Malory. J. M.
Dent & Co. 300 copies on Dutch hand-made paper
and 1500 ordinary copies. Issued in Parts, beginning
June 1893.

i. Vol. I., 1893. Frontispiece—"How King Arthur saw the Questing Beast, and thereof had great marvel." Photogravure.

Full-page illustrations :—

*ii. Merlin taketh the child Arthur into his keeping. (Reduced reproduction in *Idler*, May 1898.)

*iii. The Lady of the Lake telleth Arthur of the sword Excalibur.

*iv. Merlin and Nimue.

*v. Arthur and the strange mantle.

*vi. How four queens found Launcelot sleeping. (Property of A. E. Gallatin, Esq.)

*vii. Sir Launcelot and the witch Hellawes. (Property of A. E. Gallatin, Esq.)

*viii. How la Beale Isoud nursed Sir Tristram.

*ix. How Sir Tristram drank the love drink.

*x. How la Beale Isoud wrote to Sir Tristram.

*xi. How King Mark found Sir Tristram sleeping.

*xii. How Morgan le Fay gave a sword to Sir Tristram.

*xiii. Vol. II., 1894. Frontispiece—"The achieving of the Sangreal." Photogravure. (This was the first design executed for the work.)

Full page and double page illustrations :—

*xiv. How King Mark and Sir Dinadan heard Sir Palomides making great sorrow and mourning for la Beale Isoud (double page).

*xv. La Beale Isoud at Joyous Gard (double page).

*xvi. How Sir Launcelot was known by Dame Elaine (full page).

*xvii. How a devil in woman's likeness would have tempted Sir Bors (double page).

*xviii. How Queen Guenever rode on maying (double page).

*xix. How Sir Bedivere cast the sword Excalibur into the water (full page).

*xx. How Queen Guenever made her a nun (full page).

In the two volumes there are altogether 548 ornaments, chapter-headings, borders, initials, tail-pieces, etc.; but some of them are repetitions of the same design, others reproductions of the same design in two different sizes. (Two of these are in the Victoria and Albert Museum. Eight belong to Pickford Waller, Esq. Others are the property of Hon. Gerald Ponsonby, R. C. Greenleaf, Esq., W. H. Jessop, Esq., M. H. Sands, Esq., Robert Ross, Esq., and Messrs Carfax & Co.)

*xxi. Chapter-heading, a dragon, with conventional foliage spray branching into marginal ornaments; printed, but not published in the book.

*xxii. Initial letter J with guardian griffins; pen-and-ink, $5\frac{1}{2} \times 3\frac{1}{2}$ inches.

*xxiii. Unfinished border design, first published in "Whistler's Art Dicta and Other Essays" by A. E. Gallatin (Boston, U.S.A., and London, 1903). (Property of A. E. Gallatin, Esq.)

xxiv. Original study, approved by the publisher, for wrappers of serial issue of the "Morte Darthur," yellowish green water-colour on white paper, $10\frac{1}{4} \times 8\frac{1}{4}$ inches. This design, comprising lilies, differs from that which was finally produced by the artist and published (next item). (Property of Aymer Vallance, Esq.) 1893.

Design for wrappers of serial issue, in black on grey paper, in two states, the earlier or trial-state, having blank spaces for the lettering, only the title being given as "La Mort Darthure."

xxv. Design in gold on cream-white cloth cases of the bound volumes.

Nineteen of the above designs were republished in "A Book of Fifty Drawings," and again in "Later Work," including full-size reproductions of the following, which had suffered through excessive reduction in the published "Morte Darthur."

*xxvi. Merlin (in a circle), facing list of illustrations in Vol. I. The same reproduced in *The Idler*, March 1897.

*xxvii. Vignette of Book I., chapter xiv. Landscape with piper in a meadow and another figure in the sky.

*xxviii. Vignette of Book III., chapter iii. Three swans swimming.

*xxix. Vignette of Book V., chapter x. Nude woman rising out of the sea, holding in one hand a sword, in the other a rose.

60. PALL MALL MAGAZINE, JUNE 1893.

i. Of a Neophyte, and how the Black Art was revealed unto him by the Fiend Asomuel. Full-page illustration in pen and ink. Asomuel, meaning insomnia, was a neologism of the artist's own devising, made up of the Greek *alpha* privative, the Latin *somnus*, and the Hebrew *el*, for termination analogous to that of other spirits' names, such as Gabriel, Raphael, Azrael, etc., reproduced in "Early Work," July 1893.

ii. The Kiss of Judas. Full-page illustration in pen-and-ink. Reproduced in "Early Work."

61. LA COMÉDIE AUX ENFERS, pen and ink, published in "Modern Illustration," by Joseph Pennell. (G. Bell & Sons, 1895.) Imp. 16mo. 1893.

62. i. EVELINA, by Frances Burney. (Dent & Co., 1894.) Design in outline for title-page.

ii. EVELINA AND HER GUARDIAN, design for illustration, pen and ink and wash, $6\frac{7}{8} \times 4\frac{7}{8}$ (exclusive of marginal lines), not published.

iii. Another illustration for the same, "Love for Love," a wash drawing, $7\frac{1}{2} \times 5\frac{1}{4}$, unpublished. 1893.

63. VIRGILIUS THE SORCERER. David Nutt, 1893. Frontispiece to the large paper copies only. Reproduced in "Early Work."

64. THE LANDSLIP, frontispiece to "Pastor Sang," being William Wilson's translation of Björnson's drama, "Over Ævne." Longmans & Co., 1893. A black and white design, in conscious imitation of Albert Dürer, as the peculiar form of the signature A. B.

shows, the only occasion on which the artist employed this device. Reproduced in "Early Work." (Property of Messrs Shirley & Co., Paris.)

65. BON MOTS. 3 VOLUMES. DENT & CO., 1893.

* I. Title-page reproduced in "Later Work."

II. Figure with fool's bauble, and another small ornament for the cover.

* III. 208 grotesques and other ornaments in the three volumes. Some of these, however, are repeated, and some printed in different sizes. Three of them reproduced in "Later Work." In an article by Max Beerbohm in the *Idler*, May 1898, accompanied by "some drawings that have never before been reproduced," are nine small vignettes of the "Bon Mots" type, of which number three only are explicitly ascribed to "Bon Mots." (A sheet of them belongs to W. H. Jessop, Esq. Nineteen are the property of Pickford Waller, Esq.)

66. FOLLY, intended for "Bon Mots," but not used in the book. The figure is walking along a branch of hawthorn, the left hand upraised, and holding the fool's baton; a flight of butterflies in lower left-hand corner; with drawing 8 × 5¼ inches. (Property of Littleton Hay, Esq.)

67. PAGAN PAPERS, a volume of Essays by Kenneth Grahame. Elkin Mathews and John Lane, 1893. Title-page, design for.

68. ADA LUNDBERG, head and shoulders to right, coloured crayons on brown paper. Reproduced in colour in "Later Work." (Property of Julian Sampson, Esq.)

69. KEYNOTES SERIES OF NOVELS AND SHORT STORIES.— (The publication of this series was begun by Messrs Elkin Mathews and John Lane, and afterwards continued by Mr John Lane alone.)

I. Keynotes by George Egerton, 1893. Title-page design (the same employed for the cloth cover). Ornamental key, embodying the author's monogram, on back of "Contents" page (the same device on the back of the book). This plan was adopted for each volume of the series.

II. The Dancing Faun, by Florence Farr (the Faun in the design has the eyeglass and features of J. McNeill Whistler).

III. Poor Folk. Translated from the Russian of F. Dostoievsky, by Lena Milman.

IV. A Child of the Age, by Francis Adams.

V. The Great God Pan and the Inmost Light, by Arthur Machen, also unfinished sketch in pencil upon the back of the finished design.

VI. Discords, by George Egerton.

VII. Prince Zaleski, by M. P. Shiel.

VIII. The Woman who Did, by Grant Allen.

IX. Women's Tragedies, by H. D. Lowry, 1895.

X. Grey Roses, by Henry Harland.

XI. At the First Corner, and other Stories, by H. B. Marriott Watson.

XII. Monochromes, by Ella D'Arcy.

XIII. At the Relton Arms, by Evelyn Sharp.

XIV. The Girl from the Farm, by Gertrude Dix.

XV. The Mirror of Music, by Stanley V. Makower.

XVI. Yellow and White, by W. Carlton Dawe.

XVII. The Mountain Lovers, by Fiona Macleod.

XVIII. The Woman who Didn't, by Victoria Crosse.

XIX. Nobody's Fault, by Netta Syrett.

XX. The Three Impostors, by Arthur Machen.

XXI. The British Barbarians, a hill-top novel, by Grant Allen.

XXII. Platonic Affections, by John Smith. Design for wrapper of "Keynotes" series. John Lane, 1896.

(With the exception of No. 2 all the above Keynotes designs are the property of John Lane, Esq.)

70. THE BARBAROUS BRITISHERS, a tip-top novel, by H. D. Traill. Title-page design (the same employed for the cloth cover), comprising a portrait of Miss Ada Lundberg, the whole being a parody of the design for "The British Barbarians," *vide supra*. John Lane, 1896. (Property of John Lane, Esq.) Reproduced in "Early Work."

71. THREE HEADPIECES, two of which appeared in *St Paul's*, April 2nd, 1898, the other in the same paper, April 9th, 1898. All three republished in "Early Work." (Property of Henry Reichardt, Esq.) 1893-4.

72. WOMEN REGARDING A DEAD MOUSE. Three-quarter figure in leaden grey. Unfinished painting in oils, the only experiment the artist ever made in this medium; influenced by Walter Sickert. *c.* 1894.

73. MENU OF THE TENTH ANNUAL DINNER OF THE PLAY-GOERS' CLUB IN LONDON. Two drawings, one of them only reproduced in "Early Work." January 28th, 1894.

*74. LUCIAN'S TRUE HISTORY. Laurence & Bullen, privately printed, 1894. Black and white illustrations to

I. A Snare of Vintage. Reproduced in "Later Work."

Another drawing of the same subject and title, but different rendering, 6 × 4½ inches, was inserted loose in large paper copies only; not noted in "Contents" page of the book.

II. Dreams. Reproduced in "Later Work." This drawing was executed obviously at the same period as "Siegfried" and "The Achieving of the Sangreal."

*III., IV. Two more drawings, intended for the same work, but not included in it. Twenty copies of each were printed privately. One of them is unpublished; of the other, the upper portion was published in "Later Work." These illustrations were the earliest of the Artist's designs not intended for public circulation.

LUCIAN'S TRUE HISTORY, translated by Francis Hickes, illustrated by William Strang, J. B. Clark, and Aubrey Beardsley, with an Introduction by Charles Whibley, was published by A. H. Bullen. London, 1902.

75. QUILP'S BARON VERDIGRIS. Black and white. Designed

for Messrs Henry & Co. First published in " Second Book " and again in " Later Work." 1894.

76. POSTER FOR " THE COMEDY OF SIGHS," by Dr John Todhunter, at the Avenue Theatre, March 29th, 1894. Three-quarter length figure of woman in deep blue, standing behind a gauze curtain with light green round spots powdered over it, $28\frac{3}{4} \times 4\frac{3}{4}$ inches. The same has since been printed, the original size, in black and white. The same reduced, and printed in blue on light green paper for the programme sold in the theatre : also printed in black on toned paper for the programme of Mr G. Bernard Shaw's play, " Arms and the Man," April 21st, 1894. Also still further reduced, in black on pale mauve-pink paper for the wrapper of Mr W. B. Yeats's play, " The Land of Hearts' Desire." Reproduced in *Idler* magazine, March 1897; again in " Fifty Drawings," also in " Later Work." This was Aubrey Beardsley's first poster design. 1894.

*77. POSTER FOR MR FISHER UNWIN'S " PSEUDONYM LIBRARY." Female figure in salmon-pink dress standing on the opposite side of the road to a second-hand book-store. The scheme of colouring—salmon-pink, orange, green, and black — was suggested to Aubrey Beardsley by a French poster. $29\frac{1}{2} \times 13$ inches.

The same reduced, in colours, to form an advertisement slip for insertion in books and magazines.

The same reduced, printed in black, 6 copies only, on Japanese vellum. Reproduced in " Fifty Drawings " and " Later Work." Also used as cover-design for the " Dream and the Business," by John Oliver Hobbes.

Similar motif, black and white drawing ; exhibited at the New English Art Club Exhibition at the New Gallery. (Property of T. Fisher Unwin, Esq.)

78. POSTER FOR MR FISHER UNWIN'S CHILDREN'S BOOKS. Woman reading while seated in a groaning-chair ; black and purple. Reproduced in black in " Fifty, Drawings " and " Later Work."

79. Poster Design. A lady and large sunflower, scheme of colouring purple and yellow. Unpublished. Purchased by Mr Fisher Unwin and destroyed accidentally in New York.

80. SKETCH PORTRAIT OF THE ARTIST, head and shoulders, three-quarter face to left ; in imaginary costume with V-shaped opening to his coat and high-shouldered sleeves ; in charcoal. First published in *The Sketch*, April 14th, 1894, again in " Early Work."

81. SKETCH PORTRAIT OF HENRY HARLAND, head and shoulders, three-quarter face to right, in charcoal. First published in *The Sketch*, April 11th, 1894, again in " Early Work." (Property of John Lane, Esq.)

82. PORTRAIT OF JAMES M'NEILL WHISTLER. (Property of Walter Sickert, Esq.)

83. THE FAT WOMAN (a caricature of Mrs Whistler). First published in *To-Day*, May 12th, 1894, afterwards republished in " Fifty Drawings " and " Later Work ";

also in *Le Courrier Français*, November 11th, 1894, with the title " *Une Femme bien Nourrie*." (Formerly the property of the late Mrs Cyril Martineau (Miss K. Savile Clarke)).

84. WAITING, a haggard, expectant woman, wearing V-necked bodice and large black hat, seated in a restaurant, with a half-emptied wine-glass on a small round table before her ; black-ink drawing, $7\frac{3}{8} \times 3\frac{1}{2}$ inches, unpublished. (Property of Pickford Waller, Esq.)

85. MASKED PIERROT AND FEMALE FIGURE, water and gondolas in background, small square in black and white, published in *To-Day*, May 12th, 1894.

86. SALOME, A tragedy in one act. Translated by Lord Alfred Douglas from the French of Oscar Wilde. Elkin Mathews and John Lane, 1894. Pictured with the following designs by Aubrey Beardsley :—

* I. The woman (or man) in the moon (Frontis-piece).
Border Design for Title-page (two states, the first cancelled). Property of John Lane, Esq.)
Border Design for List of Pictures. (Property of John Lane, Esq.)
* II. The Peacock Skirt. (Property of John Lane, Esq.)
* III. The Black Cape. A burlesque, substituted for a drawing of John and Salome, which was printed but withheld, and subsequently published in " Early Work." (Property of John Lane, Esq.)
* IV. A Platonic Lament. (Property of John Lane, Esq.)
* V. Enter Herodias (two states, the first cancelled). (The drawing in its original state the property of Herbert J. Pollit Esq.) A proof of this drawing in its first state, now the property of Frank Harris, Esq., is inscribed by the artist on the left-hand top corner :

" Because one figure was undressed
This little drawing was suppressed.
It was unkind, but never mind,
Perhaps it all was for the best."

* VI. The Eyes of Herod. (Note one of Herod's white peacocks.) (Property of John Lane, Esq.)
* VII. The Stomach Dance. (The author makes Salome dance, barefooted, the Dance of the Seven Veils.) (Property of John Lane, Esq.)
* VIII. The Toilette of Salome. Substituted for a former drawing of the same subject, printed in two states but withheld, the second state subsequently published in " Early Work " (Property of Robert Ross, Esq.)
* IX. The Dancer's Reward. (Property of John Lane, Esq.)
* X. The Climax. This is a revised and simpler version of the design which had appeared in the first number of *The Studio*.
Tailpiece. The corpse of Salome being coffined

in a puff-powder box. (Property of John Lane, Esq.)

Nos. I., IV., V., and VI. of the above contain caricatures of Oscar Wilde.

*XI. Small design, printed in gold on cloth, front cover of "Salome"; another, consisting of an elaboration of the artist's device, for the under side of cover.

*XII. Study of a design of peacock feathers for cover of "Salome," not used at the time, but subsequently reproduced for the first time in facsimile in "Early Work," and again as an illustration following the title-page in reissue of "Salome" (John Lane, 1907); also in gold on light green cloth for ornament of the binding, and in olive green on orange-red for the paper cap. Also in gold on blue cloth for binding of "Under the Hill," 1904. (Property of John Lane, Esq.) This (1907) edition, moreover, contains the two illustrations suppressed in the original edition, viz., "John and Salome" (Property of John Lane, Esq.), now placed in order as No. 8, and "The Toilet of Salome, II.," now placed as No. 13 (Property of John Lane, Esq.) and an original title-page.

XIII. The Salome drawings were reproduced the actual size of the originals and published in a portfolio. In this was included a design of Salome seated upon a settee. Described in "Early Work" as "Maitresse d'Orchestre." (John Lane, 1907.)

87. DANCER WITH DOMINO. (The property of His Honour Judge Evans.)

88. PLAYS, BY JOHN DAVIDSON. Elkin Mathews and John Lane, 1894. Design on frontispiece to, containing portrait caricatures of Sir Augustus Harris, and Oscar Wilde and Henry Harland, black and white; the same design in gold on the cloth cover. Reproduced in "Early Work," and again, with Aubrey Beardsley's letter to the *Daily Chronicle* on the subject, in "Under the Hill," 1904. (Property of John Lane, Esq.)

Design for Title-Page of the above-named. Black and white; reproduced in "Early Work."

89. THE YELLOW BOOK, 1894 AND 1895.

*I. Design for prospectus of the "Yellow Book": a woman examining books in a box at a bookstall; black on yellow paper. Elkin Mathews and John Lane, 1894. (Property of John Lane, Esq.)

Vol. I., April 1894. Elkin Mathews and John Lane.

*II. Design on front side of yellow cover. (Property of John Lane, Esq.)

III. Design on under side of cover; the same repeated in the later volumes. (Property of John Lane, Esq.)

IV. Design on title-page: a woman playing a piano in a meadow. Reproduced, with Aubrey Beardsley's

letter on the subject, to the *Pall Mall Budget*, in "Under the Hill" (1904). (Property of John Lane, Esq.)

V. L'Education Sentimentale: in line and wash.

VI. Night Piece.

*VII. Portrait of Mrs Patrick Campbell in profile, to left in outline. Formerly in possession of Oscar Wilde, now in National Gallery at Berlin.

VIII. Bookplate (designed in 1893) for John Lumsden Propert, Esq.

Vol. II., July 1894. Elkin Mathews and John Lane.

IX. Design on front side of cover. (Property of John Lane, Esq.)

X. Design on title-page.

*XI. The Comedy-Ballet of Marionettes. Three designs.

*XII. Garçons de Café. (Property of A. W. King, Esq.)

*XIII. The Slippers of Cinderella. The artist subsequently coloured the original with scarlet and green, in which state it is unpublished. (Property of Brandon Thomas, Esq.)

XIV. Portrait of Madame Réjane, full-length profile to left, in outline. (Property of Frederick H. Evans, Esq.)

Volume III., October 1894. John Lane.

*XV. Design on front side of cover. (Property of John Lane, Esq.)

*XVI. Design on title-page.

*XVII. Portrait of Mantegna. Published, for a practical joke, in the name of Philip Broughton. (Property of G. Bernard Shaw, Esq.)

*XVIII. Portrait of the artist; fancy portrait of himself in bed. (Property of John Lane, Esq.)

*XIX. Lady Gold's Escort. (Property of Brandon Thomas, Esq.)

*XX. The Wagnerites at the performance of "Tristan und Isolde." Reproduced, on large scale, in *Le Courrier Français*, December 23rd, 1894, with the title "Wagnériens et Wagnériennes."

*XXI. La Dame aux Camélias. Reprinted in *St Paul's*, April 2nd, 1894, with the title "Girl at her Toilet." (Formerly the property of the late Miss K. Savile Clarke [Mrs Cyril Martineau].)

XXII. From a pastel; half-length study of a woman in white cap, facing to left. (Published, for a practical joke, in the name of Albert Foschter.)

Volume IV., January 1895. John Lane.

XXIII. Design on front side of cover.

XXIV. Design on title-page.

*XXV. The Mysterious Rose Garden, burlesque Annunciation. (Property of John Lane, Esq.)

XXVI. The Repentance of Mrs ——. (The kneeling figure is a reminiscence of the principal one in "The Litany of Mary Magdalen.")

xxvii. Portrait of Miss Winifred Emery (outline). (Property of Mrs Cyril Maude.)

* xxviii. Frontispiece for Juvenal. Double-page supplement.

* xxix. Design for "Yellow Book" Cover, not used. First published in "Early Work." (Property of John Lane, Esq.)

xxx. Show-card to advertise "The Yellow Book"; female figure standing, her hat hanging from her right hand, and daffodils growing at her feet. Dark green on light yellow paper. Reproduced in black-and-white in "Early Work." (The property of John Lane, Esq.)

90. PORTRAIT OF RÉJANE wearing a broad-brimmed hat with dark bow in front, head and shoulders, full face slightly to left, wash drawing. Reproduced by Swan Electric Engraving Company for the "Yellow Book," but not used. Unpublished.

* 91. RÉJANE, black-and-white design of the actress standing, half length, fan in hand, against a white curtain with conspicuous tassel. First published in "Second Book," and again, in a reduced state, as "Title-page ornament, hitherto unpublished" in "Early Work." 1893-4.

92. MADAME RÉJANE, full-length portrait sketch, ink and wash. First published in "Second Book," again in "Later Work."

93. MADAME RÉJANE, profile to left; sitting, legs extended, on a sofa, ink and wash. First published in "Pen Drawing and Pen Draughtsmen," by Joseph Pennell (Macmillan, 1894), again in "Fifty Drawings," and in the Idler Magazine, March 1897.

94. RÉJANE, portrait head in profile to left, in red crayon and black ink, $7\frac{1}{2} \times 6$ inches. First published in facsimile in The Studio, May 1898, again in "Later Work." (Property of Frederick H. Evans, Esq.) 1894.

95. A POSTER DESIGN. Back view of a woman, her face in profile to right, holding a pigmy in her right hand. First published in "Early Work." (Property of John Lane, Esq.)

96. A POSTER DESIGN (Singer). Woman seated at a piano. First reproduced in The Poster, October 1898, again in "Second Book" and in "Later Work."

97. LADY TO RIGHT GAZING AT A HAT ON A MILLINER'S BONNET STAND, headpiece for the "Idlers' Club" section in the Idler Magazine, 1894.

98. PIERROT AND BLACK CAT, small square in black-and-white for a book ornament.

99. HEAD AND SHOULDERS OF A CHINESE PRIEST, together with the Head of a Satyr. 25 copies only printed on folio sheet, and 10 copies only in red. It is not known for what they were intended. Published by James Tregaskis, Caxton Head.

100 LES PASSADES, night scene, in pen-and-ink with ink wash, 10×5 inches. First published in To-Day, November 17, 1894, again in the Idler Magazine, March 1897.

* 101. VENUS BETWEEN TERMINAL GODS. Frontispiece for a version of the Tannhäuser legend, to be published by Messrs H. Henry & Co. Ltd., a project never completed. Design in black-and-white, showing, especially in the treatment of flying dove and of the background of rose-trellis, the influence of Charles Ricketts or Laurence Housman. Reproduced in "Second Book," and again in "Later Work." Circa 1894-5.

102. FRONTISPIECE AND TITLE-PAGE, together forming one complete design, for "The Story of Venus and Tannhäuser," to be published by John Lane, but never completed. (Cf. "Under the Hill" in The Savoy, 1896.) Reproduced in "Early Work." Dated 1895. (Property of John Lane, Esq.)

* 103. THE RETURN OF TANNHÄUSER TO VENUSBERG. A design originally intended for the above-named book. Subsequently presented by the artist to J. M. Dent, Esq. First published, in illustration of an article by Max Beerbohm, in the Idler Magazine for May 1898, and again, in larger format and, as the initials in left hand corner show, reversed, in "Second Book" and again in "Later Work." The Idler version has a slight effect of half-tone in the brambles in the foreground, but the "Later Work" reproduction is pure black-and-white contrast.

104. VENUS. Design for title-page, in black-and-white. First published in The Studio, 1898, and afterwards in "Early Work," March 2, 1899, where it is described as "hitherto unpublished." (The property of John Lane, Esq.)

105. DESIGN FOR COVER OF "THE CAMBRIDGE A, B, C." Reproduced in "Early Work."

106. PIERROT AS CADDIE, Golf Club Card, designed for the opening of The Prince's Ladies' Golf Club, Mitcham, pen-and-ink. Published in "Early Work." (Formerly the property of Mrs Falconer-Stuart, now of R. Hippesley Cox, Esq.) Dated 1894.

107. A POSTER DESIGN; two female figures drawn in black-and-white for Mr William Heinemann. Reproduced in "Early Work."

108. THE LONDON GARLAND, published by the Society of Illustrators, 1895. A pen-and-ink drawing of a female figure in very elaborated dress reaching from her neck to the ground, intended to represent a ballet-dancer with a costume as prescribed by Mrs Grundy. The original drawing, unfinished, contains another figure, not reproduced, on the left. The original title for this drawing was "At a Distance." Reproduced in "Second Book." (Property of Joseph Pennell, Esq.)

109. AUTUMN. Design in black-and-white for a calendar to be published by William Heinemann. Reproduced in "Early Work."

110. TALES OF MYSTERY AND WONDER, by Edgar Allen Poe (Stone & Kimball, Chicago, U.S.A., 1895); four designs in pen-and-ink for large paper edition of—
    I. The Murders in the Rue Morgue.
    II. The Black Cat.
    III. The Masque of the Red Death. First published in the "Chap Book" (Chicago), Aug. 15, 1894, again in same, April 1, 1898.
    IV. The Fall of the House of Usher.

111. OUTLINE PORTRAIT OF THE ARTIST in profile to left; in imaginary costume, with a lace ruff to the neck, and earrings in the ears. Published in "Posters in Miniature," and again in "Early Work." A half-tone block from variant of the same, the earring as well as the button on lappel and waist of coat more pronounced, was published in The Hour, March 27, 1895, and reproduced in Magazine of Art, November 1896.

*112. A CHILD STANDING BY ITS MOTHER'S BED, black-and-white, chiefly outline. First published in The Sketch, April 10, 1895. Reproduced in "Early Work." Formerly in the possession of Max Beerbohm, Esq., but since lost.

*113. THE SCARLET PASTORALE, pen-and-ink. First published in The Sketch, April 10, 1895. Also printed in scarlet on white. Reproduced in "Fifty Drawings."

114. PORTRAIT OF MISS ETHEL DEVEREUX, pencil drawing. (Property of Mrs Roy Devereux.) Circa 1895.

115. DESIGN FOR AN INVITATION CARD, ink outline; seated Pierrot smoking, a copy of the "Yellow Book," Vol. IV., on the couch at his side. Drawn for Mr John Lane's Sette of Odd Volumes Smoke. Reproduced in The Studio, September 1895. (Property of John Lane, Esq.)

116. THREE DECORATIVE DESIGNS from the brown paper cover of Aubrey Beardsley's own copy of "Tristan und Isolde." Two reproduced in "Later Work." (Property of Frederick H. Evans, Esq.)

117. MAX ALVARY AS "TRISTAN" in Wagner's opera "Tristan und Isolde," half-length profile to left, pen-and-ink and wash with unusual monogram signature. 10 × 5½ inches. First published in "Aubrey Beardsley's Drawings, a catalogue and a list of criticisms," by A. E. Gallatin (New York, 1903). (Formerly the property of Rev. G. H. Palmer, now of A. E. Gallatin, Esq.)

118. FRAU KLAFSKY AS "ISOLDE" in above-named opera, pen-and-ink and pale green water-colour, 13 × 4¾ inches. First published in the Critic (New York), December, 1902. (Formerly the property of Rev. G. H. Palmer, now of A. E. Gallatin, Esq.)

*119. ISOLDE; autolithograph in scarlet, grey, green, and black on white; supplement to The Studio, October 1895.

*120. WOMAN RECLINING IN A MEADOW BY THE BORDER OF A LAKE, LISTENING TO A FAUN READING OUT OF A BOOK TO HER. Oblong design in ink on white; a variant of the design for wrapper of Leonard Smithers' Catalogue, No. 3. First published in The Studio, May 1898, again in "Early Work," where it is described as

"hitherto unpublished." (Property of John Lane, Esq.) 1895.

121. DESIGN FOR WRAPPER OF "CATALOGUE OF RARE BOOKS," No. 3. (Leonard Smithers, September 1895.) The same figures as in the last-named, but the landscape has an urn and additional trees to adapt the design to upright shape. Black on pale blue-green paper.

122. CHOPIN BALLADE III., illustration for. Woman rider, mounted on a prancing white horse to left. Wash drawing. First published in The Studio, May 1898, in half tones of grey, with deep purplish black; again in "Second Book." (Property of Charles Holme, Esq.) 1895.

123. CHOPIN'S NOCTURNES, frontispiece to. Pen-and-ink and wash. First published in "Early Work." (Property of John Lane, Esq.)

*124. EARL LAVENDER, by John Davidson (Ward & Downey, 1895), design for frontispiece to. Woman scourging a kneeling, barebacked figure. Pen-and-ink outline. Reproduced in "Early Work." (Property of John Lane, Esq.)

125. YOUNG OFEG'S DITTIES, by George Egerton (John Lane, 1895), title-page and cover design for.

*126. MESSALINA, with another woman on her left, black-and-white, with black background. First published in "Second Book," again in "Early Work," where it is described as "hitherto unpublished." 1895.

127. TITLE-PAGE ORNAMENT, standing nude figure playing double-bass, black background. First published in "Early Work."

128. PORTRAIT OF MISS LETTY LIND in "The Artist's Model." Pen-and-ink outline. Published in "Early Work." (Property of Miss Letty Lind.)

129. ATALANTA IN CALYDON, full-length figure to right; pen-and-ink and wash. First published in "Early Work." (Property of John Lane, Esq.)

130. COVER DESIGN FOR FAIRY TALES by Count Hamilton, to be published by Messrs H. Henry & Co., Ltd.

131. BALZAC'S "LA COMÉDIE HUMAINE," design (head, full face) for front side and another for the reverse of cover. Reproduced in "Later Work."

132. THE BROOK TRILLS OF PERNICIOUS BY RICHARD LE PHILISTIENNE, title-page to burlesque, that of "The Book Bills of Narcissus," by Richard le Gallienne. Unpublished. (Property of J. M. Dent, Esq.)

133. A SELF-PORTRAIT, grotesque outline profile to left, with diminutive silk hat, from the fly-leaf of an envelope in the possession of J. M. Dent, Esq. Unpublished.

134. THE SHAVING OF SHAGPAT, by George Meredith, small sketch to illustrate, in pen-and-ink, contained in a letter to Frederick H. Evans, Esq. Unpublished.

135. AN EVIL MOTHERHOOD, by Walt Ruding (Elkin Mathews, 1896), frontispiece to. Pen-and-ink. Reproduced in "Early Work."

136. Café Noir. Another design for the frontispiece of the last-named book, pen-and-ink and wash; bound up in six review copies only, and then recalled. Reproduced in " Early Work." (Property of M. Jean Ruelle.)

137. Title-page, an architectonic design. First published as the title of " Early Work " (John Lane, 1899). (Property of John Lane, Esq.)

138. Ornamental Title-page for "The Parade." Messrs H. Henry & Co., Ltd., 1896. Reproduced in " Later Work."

139. Tail-piece to Catalogue of Lord Carnarvon's Library, 1896.

140. Sappho, by H. T. Wharton. (John Lane, 1896.) Design for cover in gold on blue. Reproduced in " Early Work." (Property of John Lane, Esq.)

*141. Pierrot's Library. (John Lane, 1896.) Design for title-page of, two designs for end papers, printed in olive green; design for front cover and vignette for reserve cover, printed in gold on red cloth. Reproduced in " Early Work." (Property of John Lane, Esq.)

142. Love Enshrined in a Heart in the Shape of a Mirror, pen-and-ink. First published in " Aubrey Beardsley " by Arthur Symons. (Sign of the Unicorn, 1898.) (Property of André Raffalovich, Esq.)

143. The Lysistrata of Aristophanes. (Leonard Smithers, privately printed, 1896.) Eight pen-and-ink designs to illustrate—
    *i. Lysistrata.
    *ii. The Toilet of Lampito.
    *iii. Lysistrata haranguing the Athenian Women.
    *iv. Lysistrata defending the Acropolis.
    *v. Two Athenian Women in Distress.
    *vi. Cinesias soliciting Myrrhina.
    *vii. The Examination of the Herald.
    *viii. The Lacedemonian Ambassadors.
        An expurgated version of No. 3 was published in " Second Book," and was repeated together with expurgated versions or fragments from the remainder of the set in " Later Work."

144. The Rape of the Lock, by Alexander Pope. An heroi-comical poem in five cantos, "embroidered with nine drawings by Aubrey Beardsley," 4to. Leonard Smithers, 1896. Now published by John Lane. (Property of Messrs Keppel, New York.)
    *i. The Dream.
    *ii. The Billet-Doux (vignette). Reproduced in St Paul's, April 2, 1898. (Property of Mrs Edmund Davis.)
    *iii. The Toilet.
    *iv. The Baron's Prayer.
    *v. The Barge.
    *vi. The Rape of the Lock. (The property of Messrs Keppel, New York.)
    *vii. The Cave of Spleen.
    *viii. The Battle of the Beaux and the Belles. Reproduced in the Idler, March 1897.

*ix. The New Star (cul-de-lampe).
    *Cover design for the original edition.
    *Cover design for the Bijou edition. (John Lane.) Reproduced in " Later Work."

145. Design for Wrapper of Catalogue of Rare Books, *No. 7. (Leonard Smithers, 1896.) A lady seated on a striped settee reading; a parrot on stand on the right. Black on leaden-grey paper. Reproduced in " Second Book," 1896, and " Later Work."

*146. The Prospectus of The Savoy. Design for.
    *i. A burlesque Cupid on a stage with footlights, one hand holding a copy of the book, whence it appears that the original intention was to produce the first number in December 1895. Reproduced in " Later Work." Latter part of 1895. (Property of John Lane, Esq.)
    *ii. A suppressed variant of the above, same motif reversed, only with John Bull substituted for the Cupid. Reproduced in " Later Work."
    iii. Initial letter A in the above Prospectus. Reproduced in " Later Work."
    iv. Publisher's Trade-mark for Leonard Smithers. First published in " Savoy " Prospectus. The same, name omitted, appears in " Later Work " with the title of " Siegfried," 1895.
        The Savoy, No. 1, January 1896. (Leonard Smithers.)
    *v. Cover design, in two states. The original was suppressed because it depicted too realistically the contempt of the child in the foreground for the " Yellow Book," with which the artist had recently ceased to be connected. The revised version was republished in " Fifty Drawings," and again in " Later Work." (Property of Mrs George Bealby Wright.)
    *vi. Title-page. Repeated as title-page in No. 2, and republished in " Later Work."
    vii. Drawing to face Contents. Caricature of John Bull. Republished in " Later Work."
    *viii. The Three Musicians. Illustration of the artist's poem, same title. Republished in " Fifty Drawings " and " Later Work."
    ix. Another drawing to illustrate the above, but withheld. It appeared for the first time in " A Book of Fifty Drawings," 1897. Republished in " Later Work " and " Under the Hill."
    x. Tailpiece to the above. Republished in " Later Work " and " Under the Hill."
    *xi. The Bathers (on Dieppe Beach). Republished in " Fifty Drawings " and " Later Work."
    xii. The Moska. This subject was inspired by the children's dance at the Casino, Dieppe. Republished in the Idler Magazine, March 1897, and again in " Later Work." (Property of Mrs Edmund Davis.)
    *xiii. The Abbé. This and the two designs which follow appeared as illustrations to " Under the Hill," a romantic novel, by Aubrey Beardsley. Re-

published in "Later Work." All the illustrations of "Under the Hill" reissued with text in a volume bearing same title. John Lane, 1904.

*xiv. The Toilet of Helen. Republished in "Fifty Drawings" and "Later Work."

xv. The Fruit Bearers. Republished in "Later Work."

*xvi. A large Christmas Card, in black-and-white. Madonna, with fur-edged, richly-flowered mantle. Issued together with, but not bound in, the book. Republished in "Fifty Drawings" and "Later Work."

The Savoy. No. 2. April 1896.

xvii. Cover Design. Republished in "Later Work."

*xviii. A Foot-note. (Fancy portrait of the artist.) Republished, with omissions, in "Later Work." Also adapted in gold on scarlet for cloth cover of "Second Book."

*xix. The Ecstasy of Saint Rose of Lima. Illustration of "Under the Hill." Republished in "Fifty Drawings" and "Later Work."

xx. The Third Tableau of "Das Rheingold." Republished in "Fifty Drawings" and "Later Work."
Scene reproduced from "The Rape of the Lock."

The Savoy. No. 3. July 1896.

xxi. Cover Design. Republished in "Later Work."

xxii. Title-page. Puck on Pegasus. Repeated for the title of all the succeeding numbers. Republished in "Later Work." Also, reduced, as design for title-page of "Fifty Drawings," and in gold on scarlet for the under side of cloth cover of same.

*xxiii. The Coiffing. This and the following design accompanied Aubrey Beardsley's "Ballad of a Barber." The Coiffing was republished in the *Idler* Magazine, March 1897, and in "Fifty Drawings" and "Later Work." (Property of Messrs Obach & Co.)

xxiv. A Cul-de-Lampe. Cupid carrying a gibbet. Republished in "Later Work."

The Savoy. No. 4. August 1896.

xxv. Cover Design. Republished in "Later Work."

The Savoy. No. 5. September 1896.

xxvi. Cover Design. (Signed, for a practical joke, Giulio Floriani.) Republished in "Fifty Drawings" and "Later Work."

xxvii. The Woman in White. A sketch in white on brown paper. Republished in "Fifty Drawings" and "Later Work."

The Savoy. No. 6. October 1896.

*xxviii. Cover Design; the Fourth Tableau of "Das Rheingold." Republished in "Fifty Drawings" and "Later Work."

*xxix. The Death of Pierrot. A pen-and-ink sketch. Reproduced in "Later Work." (Property of Messrs Obach & Co.)

The Savoy. No. 7. November 1896.

xxx. Cover Design. Republished in "Later Work."

*xxxi. Ave atque Vale; Catullus, Carmen C.I. Republished in "Fifty Drawings" and "Later Work."

xxxii. Tristan und Isolde. Republished in "Later Work."

The Savoy. No. 8 (the last issued). December 1896.

xxxiii. Cover Design. Republished in "Later Work." The same adapted, with the addition of heavy black bands, and is printed in green and scarlet, for small poster to advertise the completed work.

xxxiv. A Répétition of "Tristan und Isolde." Republished in "Later Work."

*xxxv. Don Juan, Sganarelle and the Beggar; from Molière's "Don Juan." Republished in "Later Work."

*xxxvi. Mrs Margery Pinchwife, from William Wycherley's "Country Wife." Republished in "Later Work."

*xxxvii. Frontispiece to "The Comedy of the Rheingold." Republished in "Later Work."

xxxviii. Flosshilde, a Rhine Maiden; to illustrate "Das Rheingold." Republished in "Later Work." (Property of Herbert J. Pollit, Esq.)

*xxxix. Erda; to illustrate "Das Rheingold." Republished in "Later Work."

*xl. Alberich; to illustrate "Das Rheingold." Republished in "Later Work." (Property of Herbert J. Pollit, Esq.)

xli. Felix Mendelssohn Bartholdy. Republished in "Later Work." (Property of Herbert J. Pollit, Esq.)

xlii. Carl Maria von Weber. Republished in "Later Work."

*xliii. Count Valmont, from "Les Liaisons Dangereuses," by Choderlos de Laclos. Republished in "Later Work."

*xliv. Et in Arcadia Ego. Republished in "Later Work."

xlv. Small ornament for the cover of bound volumes of "The Savoy."

xlvi. Sketch of a Child (young girl), unfinished, in pencil, on the reverse of "A Foot-note." First published in "Early Work." (Property of Frederick H. Evans, Esq.)

147. A Seated Figure. Unpublished design for the Savoy, occurring as a grotesque in "Bon Mots." (Property of G. D. Hobson, Esq.)

148. Verses, by Ernest Dowson (Leonard Smithers, 1896), cover design for. Reproduced in "Later Work." (Property of John Lane, Esq.)

*149. THE PIERROT OF THE MINUTE. A Dramatic Phantasy in one act. By Ernest Dowson. Leonard Smithers, 1897. (Property of John Lane, Esq.) Four designs to illustrate :—
    *I. Frontispiece.
    II. Headpiece.
    III. Initial letter P.
    *IV. Cul-de-Lampe.
Reproduced in " Second Book " and " Later Work." Cover design for the same.

*150. APOLLO PURSUES DAPHNE. (Property of Herbert J. Pollit, Esq.)

151. THE SOUVENIRS OF LEONARD, Cover design for. Printed in gold on purple. Reproduced in " Later Work." 1897.

152. THE LIFE AND TIMES OF MADAME DU BARRY, by Douglas. Leonard Smithers, 1897. Cover design for. Reproduced in " Later Work." 1897.

*153. FRONTISPIECE TO A BOOK OF BARGAINS, by Vincent O'Sullivan. Leonard Smithers, 1897. Reproduced in the *Idler*, March 1897.

*154. COVER DESIGN FOR A BOOK OF FIFTY DRAWINGS, BY AUBREY BEARDSLEY. Leonard Smithers, 1897. Reproduced in gold on scarlet cloth. Republished on a reduced scale, in black-and-white, in " Later Work."

155. SILHOUETTE OF THE ARTIST. First published as a tail-piece at the end of " Fifty Drawings." Also in *Idler* Magazine, March 1897, and in " Later Work."

*156. BOOK-PLATE OF THE ARTIST. First published in " Fifty Drawings," 1897, also in " Later Work."

*157. ALI BABA. COVER DESIGN FOR THE FORTY THIEVES.
    I. First published in " Second Book," again in " Later Work," 1901. (Property of Messrs Robson & Co.)

    II. ALI BABA IN THE WOOD. First published in " Fifty Drawings," 1897. Also in *Idler*, May 1898, and again in " Later Work."

158. ATALANTA IN CALYDON. First published in " Fifty Drawings," 1897 ; also in the *Idler* Magazine, March 1897, and again in " Later Work." (This drawing was exhibited at the Carfax Exhibition, October 1904, under the title of " Diana," 77.)

*159. MESSALINA RETURNING FROM THE BATH. Pen-and-ink and water colours. First published in " Second Book," again in " Later Work." This drawing, together with the other one of Messalina, drawn in 1895 (see *supra*), two of Bathyllus, and one representing Juvenal scourging a woman (this last, slightly altered, reproduced in " Later Work "), belongs to a series of illustrations to the *Sixth Satire* of Juvenal. Leonard Smithers, privately printed, 1897.

160. THE HOUSES OF SIN, by Vincent O'Sullivan. Leonard

Smithers, 1897. Cover design for. Reproduced in " Second Book," again in " Later Work."

161. LA DAME AUX CAMÉLIAS. Sketch in water colour to right. On the fly-leaf of a copy of the book given to the artist by M. Alexandre Dumas, fils. First published in " Second Book," again in " Later Work." 1897.

162. BOOK-PLATE FOR MISS OLIVE CUSTANCE (Lady Alfred Douglas). Reproduced in photogravure in " Early Work."

163. ARBUSCULA. Drawing in line and wash, for the *édition de luxe* of Vuillier's " History of Dancing." William Heinemann, 1897. Reproduced in photogravure ; also an early impression of the same printed in a green tint. (Property of John Lane, Esq.)

164. MADEMOISELLE DE MAUPIN, by Théophile Gautier. Leonard Smithers, 1898. Designs to illustrate :—
    I. Mademoiselle de Maupin, frontispiece, water colour. Reproduced in facsimile by Messrs Boussod, Valadon & Co., for limited edition, and, like the rest, in photogravure for ordinary edition. Reproduced as frontispiece to " Later Work."
    II. D'Albert (small design).
    *III. D'Albert in search of Ideals. (Property of Mrs George Bealby Wright.)
    *IV. The Lady at the Dressing Table. (Property of Walter Pollett, Esq.)
    *V. The Lady with the Rose.
    VI. The Lady with the Monkey. All the above reproduced in photogravure in " Later Work."

165. BEN JONSON HIS VOLPONE : OR THE FOXE. 4to. Leonard Smithers, 1898.
    *I. Design in gold on blue for the cloth cover. Same in black-and-white for opening page. Frontispiece, design in pen-and-ink.
    *II. Vignette to the Argument. Initial letter V, with column and tasselled attachments to the capital. This and the remaining designs were executed in pen and crayon.
    *III. Vignette to Act I. Initial letter V, with an elephant, having a basket of fruits on his back. (Property of Herbert J. Pollit, Esq.)
    *IV. Vignette to Act II. Initial letter S, with a monster bird, having a pearl chain attached to its head. (Property of Herbert J. Pollit, Esq.)
    *V. Vignette to Act III. Initial letter M, with seated Venus and Cupid under a canopy, between two fantastic gynæcomorphic columns. (Property of Herbert J. Pollit, Esq.)
    Vignette to Act IV. (The same as the design for Act II. repeated.)
    *VI. Vignette to Act V. Initial letter V, with a horned terminal figure of a man or satyr. (Property of Herbert J. Pollit, Esq.)

AYMER VALLANCE